As for Me
and My Family

Other Books by Florence M. Taylor

A Boy Once Lived in Nazareth
In the Morning, Bread: Devotions for the New Day
The Bridled Tongue: Bible Words about Words
Hid in My Heart: The Word of God in Times of Need
From Everlasting to Everlasting: Promises and Prayers

AS FOR ME AND MY FAMILY

FLORENCE M. TAYLOR

WORD BOOKS, PUBLISHER
Waco, Texas

Library of Congress catalog card number: 76–48532
ISBN 0–87680–512–8

Printed in the United States of America

This book is dedicated
to the memory of my dearly loved
Father and Mother
in gratitude for a childhood
so surrounded by love
that its memories are still a blessing to me
for which I am eternally grateful
to the Heavenly Father
whom they taught me to love, trust and obey

When the Israelites had finally conquered the long-promised land, Joshua, knowing that the end of his life was near, gathered them all together for his final words. After reminding them of God's marvelous goodness to them in fulfilling all His promises, he went on to urge them to revere the Lord

". . . and serve him in sincerity and truth. Put away forever the idols which your ancestors worshiped. . . . Worship the Lord alone. But if you are unwilling to obey the Lord, then decide today whom you will obey. . . . But as for me and my family, we will serve the Lord" (Josh. 24:14–15, TLB)

Contents

Preface

This book is written for two groups of people. First, for parents —especially those whose children are young enough so that the opportunity is still open to transform the family into a Christ-centered, redemptive fellowship.

God's power is equal to moving and changing the hardest heart and to adding joyous new insights even to parents who for years have been "provoking their children to wrath" (see Eph. 6:4) and have been handling them with harsh, unloving discipline. So I hope that even parents of older children may find here reassurance and confirmation of areas where they have dealt wisely with their children and God's own wisdom as provided in his Word for dealing with family stresses and strains which may be the result of their own past ignorance, selfishness, or lack of seeking and following God's guidance.

It is true, however, that the golden years when Christian parental guidance is most important, in terms of later mature fruitfulness in the lives of children, are the years of early childhood.

For this reason I hope this book may also fall into the hands of many young people *before* they become parents. I could wish that it might be given to every Christian couple at the time they are expecting their first baby.

In many group discussions and private conversations pre-

11

ceding and accompanying the writing of this book, my heart has rejoiced to feel the quick interest and genuine response of young people in their late teens and early twenties. Their comments and reactions have had a real part in shaping the book.

I am hopeful that many young readers may save themselves years of blind fumbling and experimenting if they can see before the first child comes what they are trying to do—first in their husband-wife relationship and then in their Christian family fellowship.

For any young people who *do* read this book, I feel urged to point out an important biblical directive: "Be ye not unequally yoked together with unbelievers" (2 Cor. 6:14).

This verse does not teach clannishness or exclusiveness for Christians! It is simply common-sense advice based on the obvious fact that for the highest and most fulfilling experience in the marriage relationship (and in parenthood) the man and the woman must share a deep and sincere dedication to Jesus Christ. *Every* marriage, without exception, will have stresses and strains. In these days of insecurity and impermanence in marriage, of easy and frequent divorce and casual remarriage, a shared Christian faith is the rock foundation needed upon which to build a marriage and a family according to God's plan.

This directive contains an implied warning that young people will do well to heed. It concerns dating. The qualities and characteristics that make a good husband or wife are not necessarily those that characterize a good date. Young people who are aware of this, and also of the biblical directive above, will be careful not to drift into a dangerous situation but will confine their dating to "believers only." By this simple, common-sense rule they may save themselves untold heartaches and deep frustrations in the years ahead.

Jesus' teaching to individuals about the foundation of their lives is doubly important for two entering the sanctity of marriage:

Whosoever heareth these sayings of mine, and doeth them, I will liken him unto a wise man, which built his house upon a rock:

And the rain descended, and the floods came, and the winds blew, and beat upon that house; and it fell not: for it was founded upon a rock (Matt. 7:24–25).

PART ONE

BIBLICAL FOUNDATIONS
FOR
CHRISTIAN FAMILY LIFE

1

The Holy Family

In thinking about Christian families today, we turn naturally
to the holy family. Sometimes we wish that God in his wisdom
had allowed us to know details of the early years of Jesus' life.
What little we do know, however, is helpful as we seek to
understand our own families.

Jesus and Joseph

So far as Jesus and his relationship to Joseph are concerned,
the Bible tells us little directly but a great deal by implication.

We know that before the baby's birth Joseph received his
own special word from God:

Behold, an angel of the Lord appeared to him in a dream, saying,
"Joseph, son of David, do not be afraid to take Mary as your wife; for
that which has been conceived in her is of the Holy Spirit.
"And she will bear a Son; and you shall call His name Jesus, for it
is He who will save His people from their sins" (Matt. 1:20–21, NAS).

Joseph was with Mary and the baby in the temple (see Luke
2:21–39) when Jesus was recognized first by Simeon and then
by Anna as "the Lord's Christ." "And Joseph and his mother
marvelled at those things which were spoken of him" (Luke
2:33).

17

Matthew records a second and a third heavenly vision granted Joseph:

And when they [the wise men] were departed, behold, the angel of the Lord appeareth to Joseph in a dream, saying, Arise, and take the young child and his mother, and flee into Egypt, and be thou there until I bring thee word: for Herod will seek the young child to destroy him.
When he arose, he took the young child and his mother by night, and departed into Egypt (Matt. 2:13–14).

But when Herod was dead, behold, an angel of the Lord appeareth in a dream to Joseph in Egypt,
Saying, Arise, and take the young child and his mother, and go into the land of Israel: for they are dead which sought the young child's life (Matt. 2:19–20).

Joseph also appears in Luke's story of the trip to Jerusalem when Jesus was twelve years old (see Luke 2:41–52). This is the last mention of Joseph in the Gospel narratives except for one brief reference in the account of Jesus' rejection in Nazareth:

Is not this the carpenter's son? is not his mother called Mary? and his brethren, James, and Joses, and Simon, and Judas?
And his sisters, are they not all with us? (Matt. 13:55–56).

Was Joseph alive then? Or had he died sometime between the trip to Jerusalem and the beginning of Jesus' public ministry? The Bible does not tell us. These brief glimpses are all the record holds.

This might seem scanty evidence upon which to base any opinion about the relationship of Jesus and Joseph if it were not for a significant related truth. When the mature Jesus sought to reveal to the crowds pressing around him his knowledge of God in words they could understand, his favorite description of God was in terms of the father-child relationship. In his sermon on the mount (Matt. 5–7) Jesus refers to God as Father *seventeen* times!

It is a fair assumption that only one who had experienced human fatherhood at its best could have chosen to use the father-child relationship as the prototype for the God-man relationship. Consider this familiar passage:

Or what man is there of you, whom if his son ask bread, will he give him a stone?
Or if he ask a fish, will he give him a serpent?
If ye then, being evil, know how to give good gifts unto your children, how much more shall your Father which is in heaven give good things to them that ask him? (Matt. 7:9–11).

Consider also in this connection the lovely story of the forgiving father:

A certain man had two sons:
And the younger of them said to his father, Father, give me the portion of goods that falleth to me. And he divided unto them his living.
And not many days after the younger son gathered all together, and took his journey into a far country, and there wasted his substance with riotous living.
And when he had spent all, there arose a mighty famine in that land; and he began to be in want.
And he went and joined himself to a citizen of that country; and he sent him into his fields to feed swine.
And he would fain have filled his belly with the husks that the swine did eat: and no man gave unto him.
And when he came to himself, he said, How many hired servants of my father's have bread enough and to spare, and I perish with hunger!
I will arise and go to my father, and will say unto him, Father, I have sinned against heaven, and before thee,
And am no more worthy to be called thy son: make me as one of thy hired servants.
And he arose, and came to his father. But when he was yet a great way off, his father saw him, and had compassion, and ran, and fell on his neck, and kissed him.
And the son said unto him, Father, I have sinned against heaven, and in thy sight, and am no more worthy to be called thy son.
But the father said to his servants, Bring forth the best robe, and put it on him; and put a ring on his hand, and shoes on his feet:
And bring hither the fatted calf, and kill it; and let us eat, and be merry:

For this my son was dead, and is alive again; he was lost, and is found. And they began to be merry (Luke 15:11–24).

We have said that it is a fair assumption from his relationship to God that Jesus' experience of human fatherhood was on a high level. Modern family experience bears this out, both positively and negatively. A child of a brutal, violent father cannot come to a trusting relationship with the Father-God without first going through a deep and shattering experience whereby the firmly implanted father-image of his childhood is uprooted from his mind and heart and replaced with the realization of "the Lord and Father of our Lord Jesus Christ."

Robert was in his late teens when he confided to me his personal experience:

I grew up in a family with an alcoholic father. Frequent beatings with a strap are my most vivid memories of childhood. As soon as I was old enough, I left home. For a while, I made out as best I could, but at last a much-loved pastor and his wife offered me a home with them, which I gratefully accepted.

I began going around with a girl, and I realized after a while that her loving, trustful, joyous response to God was quite different from my own experience. But when I met her father, I understood. All her experience of human fatherhood had prepared her for her relationship with God. And all *my* experience had put stumblingblocks in my way. Praise God that he is gradually removing those blocks and drawing me to him with a new trust and love and joy!

Human fathers do well to ponder this truth: One's early conception of God is almost invariably founded upon the child's idea of his or her father. Praise God indeed that this works positively as well as negatively!

Jesus and Mary

The relationship of Jesus and Mary is more clearly indicated in the Bible than that of Jesus and Joseph. There is of course, first of all, the lovely story of the Annunciation and Mary's submissive response: "Behold the handmaid of the Lord; be it unto me according to thy word" (Luke 1:38).

Luke's story of Mary's visit to her cousin Elisabeth before the child's birth includes the lovely Magnificat that begins:

My soul doth magnify the Lord,
And my spirit hath rejoiced in God my Saviour. . . .
For he that is mighty hath done to me great things; and holy is his name (Luke 1:46–47, 49).

It is easy for us to imagine the scene in the stable in Bethlehem where Mary lovingly wrapped her little newborn baby in swaddling clothes and laid him in the hay-filled manger.

We know too that Mary and Joseph conformed to the customs of their people and presented the baby in the temple (see Luke 2:22–40). We know the little family fled to Egypt (see Matt. 2:13–15) and stayed there until the death of Herod. We know they returned from Egypt and went to Nazareth; there the small toddler lived and grew.

In the story of the trip to Jerusalem, how gentle is Mary's reproach to her Son, and how loving and submissive is Jesus' reply:

Son, why has thou thus dealt with us? behold, thy father and I have sought thee sorrowing.
And he said unto them, How is it that ye sought me? wist ye not that I must be about my Father's business? . . .
And he went down with them, and came to Nazareth, and was subject unto them (Luke 2:48–49, 51).

Another incident, years later, has in it a humorous element. The occasion was the wedding at Cana (see John 2:1–11). You remember there was a shortage of wine and Mary called the attention of her Son to the host's predicament.

The mother of Jesus said unto him, They have no wine.
Jesus saith unto her, Woman, what have I to do with thee? mine hour is not yet come (John 2:3–4).

This has always seemed a little out of character, but notice

Mary's response. She did *not* say, "That's no way to speak to your mother!" She did not argue with her Son and say, "Did you hear what I said?" She did not threaten, "You do something about this—or else!" She did not coax or beg, "Look, you *must* help our host!"

She completely ignored his remark! She had absolute confidence that in spite of his words he would most certainly respond to the human need revealed. She did not even answer him! She spoke *to the servants!* "His mother saith unto the servants, Whatsoever he saith unto you, do it" (John 2:5).

And what happened? "Jesus saith unto them, Fill the waterpots with water" (John 2:7), and he performed the first of many miracles. How blessed it would be if we ordinary parents could learn Mary's secret—her ability to treat her Son with confident expectancy, focusing always on the positive goodness in him, calling forth by her steady belief in him the response of obedient love and cooperation!

A third incident is related in Mark. This is the account of the time when Mary and Jesus' brothers (perhaps concerned for Jesus' physical safety?) came seeking him.

There came then his brethren and his mother, and, standing without, sent unto him, calling him.

And the multitude sat about him, and they said unto him, Behold, thy mother and thy brethren without seek for thee.

And he answered them, saying, Who is my mother, or my brethren?

And he looked round about on them which sat about him, and said, Behold my mother and my brethren!

For whosoever shall do the will of God, the same is my brother, and my sister, and mother (Mark 3:31–35).

A rejection of his own family? Ah, no, surely not! Merely the extension of his deep love and concern to include the larger family of his heavenly Father.

Still another incident shows the tender love of Jesus for his mother. This occurred in the midst of his agony upon the cross:

Now there stood by the cross of Jesus his mother, and his mother's sister, Mary the wife of Cleophas, and Mary Magdalene.

When Jesus therefore saw his mother, and the disciple standing by, whom he loved, he saith unto his mother, Woman, behold thy son!

Then saith he to the disciple, Behold thy mother! And from that hour that disciple took her unto his own home (John 19:25–27).

One final reference to Mary is found in Acts 1. After listing the names of the disciples, the account reads: "These all continued with one accord in prayer and supplication, with the women, and Mary the mother of Jesus, and with his brethren" (Acts 1:14).

The Eldest Brother

The Bible tells us that Jesus was the eldest brother in a family but gives us very little information about his brothers and sisters. One reference comes near the beginning of his ministry:

And when he was come into his own country, he taught them in their synagogue, insomuch that they were astonished, and said, Whence hath this man this wisdom, and these mighty works?

Is not this the carpenter's son? is not his mother called Mary? and his brethren, James, and Joses, and Simon, and Judas?

And his sisters, are they not all with us? Whence then hath this man all these things?

And they were offended in him (Matt. 13:54–57).

We can only imagine, with reverent wonder, how Jesus' warm, protective love must have reached out to these small ones as one after another they took their places in the crowded little village home.

We know from accounts of his years of ministry how tender he was with all children, how his words and actions, in sharp contrast to the prevailing attitudes of his time, focused attention on the "personhood" of children, on God's concern for each tiny tot (see Matt. 18:1–6; Mark 10:13–16; Luke 18:15–17).

It is also fair to assume that Jesus knew only too well the experience of being rejected by those nearest and dearest to him. In the story above of his teaching in the Nazareth synagogue and of his rejection by his neighbors, no mention is made of any brother standing boldly by his side, choosing to share with him in this hour of disappointment and misjudgment. In this light, how deeply moving is Jesus' final comment: "A prophet is not without honour, save in his own country, and in his own house" (Matt. 13:57).

In spite of this early rejection, the time came (but perhaps not before Jesus' death and resurrection) when the eyes of his family were opened and they were counted among his followers in Jerusalem, where his brother James became an accepted leader of the early Christians.

In his Letter to the Galatians, Paul testifies to this:

But when it pleased God, . . . to reveal his Son in me, that I might preach him among the heathen; immediately I conferred not with flesh and blood:
Neither went I up to Jerusalem to them which were apostles before me; but I went into Arabia, and returned again unto Damascus.
Then after three years I went up to Jerusalem to see Peter, and abode with him fifteen days.
But other of the apostles saw I none, save James the Lord's brother (Gal. 1:15–19).

Also in Acts we read:

And when they were come in, they went up into an upper room, where abode both Peter, and James, and John, and Andrew, Philip, and Thomas, Bartholomew, and Matthew, James the son of Alphaeus, and Simon Zelotes, and Judas the brother of James.
These all continued with one accord in prayer and supplication, with the women, and Mary the mother of Jesus, and with his brethren (Acts 1:13–14).

Summary

What can we parents learn from this consideration of the holy family? Two verses, similar in content (repeated, perhaps, for emphasis?), are significant:

And the child grew, and waxed strong in spirit, filled with wisdom: and the grace of God was upon him (Luke 2:40).

And Jesus increased in wisdom and stature, and in favour with God and man (Luke 2:52).

Obviously Jesus' childhood home fulfilled his every need—physical, mental, moral (in his relationship to people), and spiritual (in his relationship to God).

It is interesting to note that psychologists today frequently speak of a child's personality in terms of mental, physical, spiritual and social development. Here, hundreds of years before a scientific study of children revealed their growth patterns, the Word of God set forth a divine pattern. And of no little significance, this divine pattern was used of the Son of God, who was true and perfect man as well as true and undiminished God.[1]

As parents our responsibility is to fulfill each child's individual needs in these four areas. God's method of meeting *our* needs, of redeeming and perfecting *us,* is through the outpouring of his never-changing, everlasting love. "We love him, because he first loved us" (1 John 4:19).

A Special Note to Fathers

Isaiah points out part of the father's responsibility: "The father to the children shall make known thy truth" (Isa. 38:19).

And this is a restatement of the important directive Moses pronounced:

Hear, O Israel: The Lord our God is one Lord:
And thou shalt love the Lord thy God with all thine heart, and with all thy soul, and with all thy might.
And these words, which I command thee this day, shall be in thine heart:
And thou shalt teach them diligently unto thy children, and shalt talk of them when thou sittest in thine house, and when thou walkest by the way, and when thou liest down, and when thou risest up (Deut. 6:4–7).

Every father needs to pray with deep earnestness that each child's experience of human fatherhood may lay a sound foundation for his relationship to "the God and Father of our Lord Jesus Christ," that he himself may fully and prayerfully accept his God-given responsibility as head and "priest" of his family, and that he may grow in his ability to function effectively in that capacity.

A Special Note to Mothers

The writer of Proverbs, in describing "a virtuous woman," said:

> She openeth her mouth with wisdom; and in her tongue is the law of kindness. . . .
> Her children arise up, and call her blessed; her husband also, and he praiseth her (Prov. 31:26, 28).

Every mother needs to pray for the kind of divine love for her husband and for each of the children that is as steady and dependable as God's gifts of sunshine and rain. She recognizes and loyally supports her husband as "head" of the family and expects always the children's obedience and cooperation. Such love is the most powerful force in all creation for the redemption and salvation of human spirits.

For Both Parents to Consider

Inculcating Christian standards is like building a fire in the rain. It requires willful determination, against all odds to do what seems impossible. It calls for expertise—know-how which understands the nature of the child and the nature of a hostile world. It demands a stubborn perseverance to keep fanning the flickering flame, to keep protecting the hot coals. A warm young life, glowing for Christ, is the most needed commodity in the damp chill of the marketplace today.[2]

Parents can hope to succeed in this most difficult and important task only with daily renewal through prayer which channels into the family fellowship the illimitable power of God himself and insures the one absolute essential in the creation of a Christian family fellowship—the presence of the living Christ.

The following prayer (the first part adapted from a prayer for the church) is beautifully appropriate for the Christian family but also reaching out to every individual drawn within its circle:

Prayer for the Family

We pray, holy Father, for Thy blessing on our home.
Here may the faithful find salvation, and the careless be awakened.
Here may the tempted find help, and the sorrowful be encouraged.
Here may the weary find rest, and the strong be renewed.
Here may the aged find consolation, and the young be inspired.
O Lord our God, Giver of life and love: Grant that we may ever seek Thy presence, that our home may be an abode of peace and love.
Bless our going out and our coming in, from this time forth;
Graciously shield and protect us from all evil;
Prosper us in all rightful undertakings;
And whether in prosperity or adversity, in health or in sickness, let us know that Thy Fatherly hand is upon us for good.
Knit us closely together in worship of Thee; through Jesus Christ our Lord. Amen.[3]

2

God's Order for the Family

Any consideration of relationships within a *Christian* family must surely grow out of a study of God's Word. What does the Bible say about God's plan for the human family?

The creation story in Genesis points out that God created man, and then, because "it was not good for man to be alone," he created woman to be man's helpmeet.

What a blessed thing it is to be a helpmeet! When a woman loves her husband and knows beyond any shadow of doubt that he loves her, how willingly she accepts the fact that God has placed him in authority as the head of the family! She rejoices that God has not given to her alone the awesome responsibility for the physical and spiritual well-being of her "flock"! What woman would want to be married to a man she could not honor and reverence? One to whom she was unable to give willing and joyous submission?

Husband and wife need to recognize the significance of these words of Jesus:

Have ye not read, that he which made them at the beginning made them male and female,

And said, For this cause shall a man leave father and mother, and shall cleave to his wife: and they twain shall be one flesh?

Wherefore they are no more twain, but one flesh. What therefore God hath joined together, let not man put asunder (Matt. 19:4–6).

When the father is recognized as the "authority," as the head of the house, by both wife and children, when he recognizes this authority as conferred on him by God and knows he is responsible to God for his use of it, when the wife respects her husband and finds joy in her helpmeet role, and when the husband loves his wife with faithful tenderness, the basic conditions for a Christian family based upon biblical directives have been met.

Wives, submit yourselves unto your own husbands, as it is fit in the Lord.
Husbands, love your wives, and be not bitter against them.
Children, obey your parents in all things: for this is well pleasing unto the Lord (Col. 3:18–20).

When the parents are in reality "one flesh" and present an undivided front to the children, when they both recognize and accept the lordship of Jesus Christ, obedience on the part of children is not difficult to secure.

Submission does not mean, on the one hand, giving in to tyrannical, heavy-handed, unloving commands, nor, on the other hand, surly, unwilling, grudging compliance. True submission grows out of loving concern for each other. Submission means, in essence, an attitude of joyous affirmation toward another person. You affirm what he is, what he says, what he does. You are on his side.

The biblical directive is clear:

Be filled with the Spirit;
Speaking to yourselves in psalms and hymns and spiritual songs, singing and making melody in your heart to the Lord;
Giving thanks always for all things unto God and the Father in the name of our Lord Jesus Christ;
Submitting yourselves one to another in the fear of God (Eph. 5:18–21).

Submission is not commanded of any one person alone. It is always a two-way street. Submission of each to all (father to wife and children, mother to husband and children, children

to parents and to each other, and each member of the family
to Christ) is God's order for the Christian family.

3

"I Came to Fulfill"

In our study of biblical teachings about family living, it is essential to recognize the relationship of the Old and New Testaments. We believe with Paul that "all scripture is given by inspiration of God, and is profitable for doctrine, for reproof, for correction, for instruction in righteousness" (2 Tim. 3:16).

It is obvious, however, that some scriptural passages are more valuable than others for those seeking light on their role as Christian parents.

Are we not on safe ground when we assume that from the beginning of time God has been revealing himself to his creatures? Through his creation of the world, through the circumstances of men's lives, through the inspired words of his prophets, through his (often unrecognized) Holy Spirit indwelling the hearts of men, little by little, God has revealed himself. During Old Testament days he was preparing the hearts of men for his perfect revelation in Jesus, the Son of his Spirit.

God, who at sundry times and in divers manners spake in times past unto the fathers by the prophets,
Hath in these last days spoken unto us by his Son, whom he hath appointed heir of all things, by whom also he made the worlds;
Who being the brightness of his glory, and the express image of his person, and upholding all things by the word of his power, when he had by himself purged our sins, sat down on the right hand of the Majesty on high (Heb. 1:1–3).

Much of the Old Testament is of permanent value. Many of its directives are as binding for us as they were for the early Hebrews to whom they were first given. Some directives, however, were given for a particular time and a particular situation. These are interesting historically but are not binding on us today.

The first five chapters of Leviticus, for instance, deal with sacrificial proceedings in the temple, but we no longer offer animal sacrifices for the remission of our sins because, as the writer of Hebrews explains, Christ has

. . . by his own blood . . . obtained eternal redemption for us.

For if the blood of bulls and of goats, and the ashes of an heifer sprinkling the unclean, sanctifieth to the purifying of the flesh:

How much more shall the blood of Christ, who through the eternal Spirit offered himself without spot to God, purge your conscience from dead works to serve the living God? (Heb. 9:12–14).

In this connection, Paul expressed a lovely insight in his Letter to the Romans: "I beseech you therefore, brethren, by the mercies of God, that ye present your bodies a living sacrifice, holy, acceptable unto God, which is your reasonable service" (Rom. 12:1).

In a similar way, Jesus frequently commented on certain Old Testament teachings in order to interpret them or to lift the teaching to a higher moral level. He said repeatedly: "Ye have heard that it hath been said . . . , *but I say unto you . . .*" On one occasion, he declared: "Think not that I am come to destroy the law, or the prophets: I am not come to destroy, but to fulfill" (Matt. 5:17).

Surely this is exactly what we should expect! John wrote:

In the beginning was the Word, and the Word was with God, and the Word was God. . . .

And the Word was made flesh, and dwelt among us, (and we beheld his glory, the glory as of the only begotten of the Father,) full of grace and truth (John 1:1, 14).

God's revelation in his Son, "the Word made flesh," completes, clarifies, and fulfills all previous revelation.

As one illustration of fulfilling an Old Testament directive, Jesus said, "Ye have heard that it hath been said, An eye for an eye, and a tooth for a tooth" (Matt. 5:38). He was, of course, recalling one of the Old Testament directives found in Exodus:

Thou shalt give life for life,
Eye for eye, tooth for tooth, hand for hand, foot for foot,
Burning for burning, wound for wound, stripe for stripe (Exod. 21:23–25; see also Lev. 24:20, Deut. 19:21).

At the time this Old Testament law was given it was actually *a limitation on revenge.* What it said in effect was: You may not do to another person *anything more* than he has done to you.

Jesus' fulfillment of this directive goes infinitely farther than *limitation:*

But I say unto you, That ye resist not evil: but whosoever shall smite thee on thy right cheek, turn to him the other also.

And if any man will sue thee at the law, and take away thy coat, let him have thy cloak also.

And whosoever shall compel thee to go a mile, go with him twain (Matt. 5:39–41).

Here we have not a *limitation* but an *absolute and total rejection of revenge*—and more. Here is a positive outreach of forgiving love, completely devoid of bitterness, resentment, and the desire for retaliation. A similar fulfillment is true in other similar teachings.

For instance:

Ye have heard that it hath been said, Thou shalt love thy neighbour, and hate thine enemy.

But I say unto you, Love your enemies, bless them that curse you,

do good to them that hate you, and pray for them which despitefully
use you, and persecute you;

That ye may be the children of your Father which is in heaven: for
he maketh his sun to rise on the evil and on the good, and sendeth rain
on the just and on the unjust (Matt. 5:43–45).

It is completely biblical for us prayerfully to follow this pattern given by Jesus: to consider Old Testament teachings or
directives in light of the life and teachings of Jesus, "God's
Word made flesh," and when we find clear justification in his
words or actions to say confidently, "We have read in the Old
Testament . . . , but Jesus Christ teaches . . ."

This approach will enable us to grapple constructively with
many Old Testament passages which may have puzzled and
deeply troubled us. Consider these verses:

Everyone that curseth his father or his mother shall be surely put to
death (Lev. 20:9).

And the man that committeth adultery with another man's wife, . . .
shall surely be put to death (Lev. 20:10).

Or consider this extreme illustration:

If a man have a stubborn and rebellious son, which will not obey
the voice of his father, or the voice of his mother, and that, when
they have chastened him, will not hearken unto them:

Then shall his father and his mother lay hold on him, and bring
him out unto the elders of his city, and unto the gate of his place;

And they shall say unto the elders of his city, This our son is stubborn and rebellious, he will not obey our voice; he is a glutton, and a
drunkard.

And all the men of his city shall stone him with stones, that he die
(Deut. 21:18–21).

No one, I presume, would recommend this way of dealing
with rebellious teenagers today even though "the Bible says
so"! But it may be a comfort to our hearts to be able to say: "We
have read in the Old Testament . . . , but Christ Jesus teaches
. . . ," and then to refresh our spirits with how Jesus "fulfilled,"

for instance, the law about the rebellious son, in his story of the forgiving father.

"Ye have heard that it hath been said . . ." Let us thank God for his partial revelation in the Old Testament and joyously and humbly submit ourselves to its teachings when we have proved and tested them by Jesus.

"But I say unto you . . ." Let us also thank God gratefully for the fulfillment of his revelation in Jesus, and let us study the Old Testament in light of the New, with Jesus, God's Word made flesh, as our final authority.

4

The Parents' Purpose

Almost thirty years ago, Dr. D. Elton Trueblood pointed out that the redemptive fellowship of Jesus and his disciples was not an accident of history. On the contrary, it seems to have been the deliberately chosen method whereby Jesus planned for the continuance after his death of his redemptive task— lifting all mankind to a new relationship with God and with one another.

The world needed a saving faith and the formula was that such a faith comes by a particular kind of fellowship. Jesus was deeply concerned for the continuation of his redemptive work after the close of his earthly existence, and his chosen method was *the formation of a redemptive society*. He did not form an army, establish a headquarters, or even write a book. All he did was to collect a few unpromising men, inspire them with a sense of his vocation and theirs, and build their lives into an intensive fellowship of affection, worship and work.[1]

Dr. Trueblood goes on to point out that this first fellowship was made up of ordinary people and that several of them displayed extraordinary weaknesses and failings. Judas was there, who, for reasons difficult to understand (even, perhaps, to Judas himself), betrayed the Master whom he loved. Peter was there, weak and cowardly even at a late point in his association with Jesus. (But Jesus transformed the vacillating,

uncertain Peter into the courageous "rock" upon which he built
his church.) James and John were there, wanting assurance of
prestige and power in the kingdom they expected Jesus to establish. Others were there in that little fellowship, so incon-
spicuous in their ordinariness that all we know of them is a list
of names, and even the lists given in Scripture show some
discrepancy (see Matt. 10:2–4; Acts 1:13).

Quite ordinary people! And yet that little group of weak and
faulty human beings was a redemptive society—first for themselves as individuals and then in ever-broadening circles outside their original fellowship. In one of the miracles of history
they justified Jesus' faith in them. They generated a spiritual
force unmatched before or since and so, against seemingly in-
surmountable odds, insured the continuation of the Christian
faith.

"The world needed a saving faith and [Jesus'] formula was
that such a faith comes by a particular kind of fellowship."
Today, as always, *our families* need a saving faith, and Jesus'
formula is still valid: Such a faith comes by a particular kind
of fellowship.

For parents this is a startling and quickening thought. Of
course, all Christian parents desire for their children a saving
and redemptive faith. It is easy, however, to assume that faith
comes in various ways—accepting certain tenets of belief, sup-
pressing all doubts and questions, submitting to various disciplines,
or performing prescribed, routine acts of religious observance.
That the Christian faith comes by a particular kind of fellowship
opens up new directions for creative action in family living.

What was the one factor in this original redemptive fellowship that determined its unique quality? The answer leaps at
us from the pages of the Gospels: *It included Jesus Christ himself.*

Make no mistake about it: No family can transform itself
into a redemptive fellowship without the recognized and continuous presence of the living Christ as its Master and Lord.

Praise be to God! That living presence is now and always
available to every seeking family. We have Jesus' own promise: "Behold, I stand at the door, and knock: if any man hear my

voice, and open the door, I will come in to him, and will sup with him, and he with me" (Rev. 3:20).

When parents recognize and accept as their true and all-inclusive purpose the transforming of their family into a Christian fellowship, the particular kind of fellowship Jesus and his disciples shared, a fellowship guided and controlled by the living spirit of Jesus Christ, several interesting insights become clear.

1. This purpose can be fulfilled only if parents have accepted Jesus as personal Lord and Master and have found the secret of living continuously in awareness of his abiding presence. Parents cannot share with their children a relationship with Jesus they do not have; nor can they lead their children into this much-to-be-desired relationship except by the persuasive reality of their own example.

2. This purpose must control every minute of every twenty-four hours, every day of the year. It is not an "additive" tacked on to an existing situation: It is the living yeast which permeates the total life.

And again he [Jesus] said, Whereunto shall I liken the kingdom of God?
It is like leaven, which a woman took and hid in three measures of meal, till the whole was leavened (Luke 13:20–21).

3. This purpose is like a clear shining light brought into a darkened room. It does away with confusion and bewilderment. It provides clear discernment in the mass of advice (often contradictory) to which a conscientious parent is exposed. Jesus said: "I am the light of the world: he that followeth me shall not walk in darkness, but shall have the light of life" (John 8:12).

4. This purpose provides a single clear and uncomplicated standard by which to test family practices and procedures. Will this particular way of living forward or obstruct the creation of a Christian family fellowship? "Prove all things; hold fast that which is good" (1 Thess. 5:21).

5. This purpose is simple and clear enough to be shared with

children at an early age. "You see, we are trying to be a *Christian* family, living as Jesus taught, and so, of course, . . ." This immediately lifts all decisions out of the area of the parents' irrational, inconsistent, "fleshly" action (and reaction!), and places them in the context of the eternal verities revealed in the Word of God.

For parents, Jesus' teaching about the vine and the branches has special meaning. It holds in it a lovely symbol of perfect family relationships: the parents a single branch (one flesh), firmly attached to the vine, through which the life of the vine flows out into each tiniest branchlet. This symbol also pictures the one and only way parents can successfully fulfill the purpose God has put in their hearts. *Only* as they are one branch, strongly and inseparably attached to the vine, can they hold the family in its God-ordained relationships to one another and to God. Jesus said:

I am the true vine, and my Father is the husbandman. . . .
Abide in me, and I in you. As the branch cannot bear fruit of itself, except it abide in the vine; no more can ye, except ye abide in me.
I am the vine, ye are the branches: He that abideth in me, and I in him, the same bringeth forth much fruit: for without me ye can do nothing (John 15:1, 4–5).

5

The Parents' Faith

It is possible that some of you reading these pages may be saying something like this to yourselves: "That's all very well for parents who have a firm faith of their own, who know what they believe, who aren't troubled by doubts and questions, but I'm not at all sure what I believe. What can I, in all honesty, pass on to my children?"

I am reminded of an incident in a play *The Music Master*. A young student was having her first interview with the old maestro, and he asked her gently, "And what do you know about music?"

Her reply came honestly and urgently, "Oh, professor, I don't know a single thing!"

And the maestro nodded his head and commented, "What a wonderful beginning!"

Recognizing a specific need can be the first step toward its fulfillment. Each of us needs to pray at many times in our struggle toward a firm and mature faith, "Lord, I believe; help thou mine unbelief" (Mark 9:24). It may be helpful to face squarely your doubts and questions. You may be surprised to discover how many people before you have come through a time of dark despair and unbelief into a joyous recognition that faith is *not* totally and blindly unreasonable, an escape from reality, a refuge for the weak and cowardly, but a firm

rock on which to stand amid perplexing and confusing circumstances.

"Is God real? Or is he just a figment of man's imagination?"
You may not, at first, find much in the Bible as a direct answer
to this question, for the Bible apparently makes no attempt to
answer this question directly. It does not argue or seek to prove
God's existence. It assumes it. It points out the evidence of his
activity and invites the reader to *experience his reality.* "O
taste and see that the Lord is good" (Ps. 34:8).

Saints in all ages have testified that when we reach out to
God it is not in reality on our own initiative but it is in response
to God's prior activity. We seek him because he first sought
us. "We love him, because he first loved us" (1 John 4:19).

Most of us may feel no great need for God when our lives
are fairly comfortable, but when tragedy comes, we are driven
to our knees. How beautifully Margueritte Harmon Bro has
expressed this almost universal experience:

> Like little streams that start from a dozen hidden places,
> Are my wandering desires to know Thee
> When my days are fair and free.
> But like a river tearing through canyons of rock
> to find the sea,
> Is my urge to find Thee
> When my days are dark with storm.[1]

In an adult education class recently, the group was studying
prayer. In one session someone quoted Hebrews 11:6: "He
that cometh to God must believe that he is."

Suddenly the discussion was interrupted as a woman broke
in urgently, "But that's not always true!" And she poured out a
recent experience when a lovingly awaited grandchild had been
born blind. "I didn't have any faith!" she declared. "All I had
was agony, but I had to pray, and I did. I said, 'God! If there
is a God, help me!'" After a moment of startled silence, she
added softly, "And he did. He honored even that prayer of
little faith."

If your faith is weak or lacking but you wish it were a strong reality, begin your search wherever you are with an honest prayer, even if it has to be "God, if you really are," and claim God's promise in his holy Word: "And ye shall seek me, and find me, when ye shall search for me with all your heart" (Jer. 29:13).

It seems to me that as we start out on a search for faith the first question we ask is: Was this world in which we find ourselves and of which we are a part "created" or did it just happen? Was it the result of purposeful, all-powerful creative spirit, or was it the result of an accidental and tremendous explosion—"a great bang"—which started all the millions of whirling orbs in motion throughout the vast immensity of space?

There are, it seems to me, only three possible answers to that question so far as our faith is concerned:

1. I believe in a creator.
2. I believe in a "big bang."
3. I don't know what I believe. (But if this is your answer, you will live as though you believed the second.)

Neither of the first two beliefs is a final answer; neither does away with the problem. Both lines of thinking ultimately end in another question, Who made God? or Where did the elements of the big explosion come from? Human knowledge can go just so far, and then it comes up against impenetrable mystery.

As for me, I choose to believe in a creator. I admit freely that I cannot prove that God exists, but I do *not* admit that there is no evidence upon which to base an honest belief in his existence.

I look at the world around me, and I see the orderly succession of "seedtime and harvest, and cold and heat, and summer and winter, and day and night" (Gen. 8:22). I see that acorns invariably grow into oak trees, that carrot seeds always grow into carrots. I marvel that of thousands of snowflakes photographed no identical two have ever been found although all are six-sided. I marvel that the honeycomb of the bees is made to a perfect and invariable pattern.

I agree wholeheartedly with the psalmist who declared:

The heavens proclaim God's splendour,
 the sky speaks of his handiwork;
day after day takes up the tale,
 night after night makes him known;
their speech has never a word,
 not a sound for the ear,
and yet the message spreads the wide world over,
 their meaning carries to earth's end (Ps. 19:1–4, Moffatt).

And then I look at people, and in people too I see evidence of divine creativity. I remember Jeremiah, speaking for God, declaring: "Yea, the stork in the heaven knoweth her appointed times; and the turtle and the crane and the swallow observe the time of their coming; but my people know not the judgment of the Lord" (Jer. 8:7).

The created universe follows the divine decree, but people, having been given free will, often choose to rebel. Admittedly, a number of people seem to be bad advertisements of the power and intelligence that created them, but they are as we should expect them to be if they had "just happened," accidentally. Then of course they would be like animals with no inner urgency except to satisfy their own needs, with a total lack of concern for anyone but themselves.

Not all people are like that however. In fact, the degraded, bestial man is recognized as being "unnatural." How much goodness and love have found their way into human life—even as it is today! There *are* tremendous efforts being made by dedicated, self-sacrificing individuals to care for the destitute, the handicapped, the weak, and, yes, even for the evil, vicious, depraved specimens of mankind. Not enough, of course, but, many such efforts are undeniably present.

And as I read history, I stand in awe before the miracles frail human beings can accomplish when they are gripped by unshakable faith in an omnipotent, omnipresent, righteous God-Creator.

In all these things I see purpose, not accident; so I choose to believe in God.

None of this, however, is distinctively *Christian* faith. It might as reasonably be the belief of a Moslem, a Buddhist, or of any one of the religious faiths prevalent in the world. For us who claim to be Christians, it becomes necessary to take a further leap of faith, to believe that "God so loved the world, that he gave his only begotten Son, that whosoever believeth in him should not perish, but have everlasting life" (John 3:16).

How do we come to that necessary leap of faith? Jesus has given us the answer in his Word:

> My doctrine is not mine, but his that sent me.
> If any man will do his will, he shall know of the doctrine, whether it be of God, or whether I speak of myself (John 7:16–17).

There it is again, the invitation to "taste and see." Are the promises of God in the Bible to be depended upon? Will God do the wonderful things he has promised? There is one way to find out—put him to the test.

After the earthquake had released Paul and Silas, the frightened jailer at Philippi cried out in fear, "Sirs, what must I do to be saved? And they said, Believe on the Lord Jesus Christ" (Acts 16:30–31).

To his faith in a Creator, the *Christian* adds belief in Jesus as God's Son. We acknowledge his lordship in our lives. He is our Savior, our Redeemer, our ever-present living Lord with whom we find ourselves led into a personal I-Thou relationship, and through him our faith in a Creator-God is deepened into a Father-child relationship.

With this faith we go back to the Bible with an awakened interest, for now we see it as God's inspired Word to *us*. We read in it the record of God's dealings with his people through long ages, of his gift to us of free will, so that we may respond to him and yield ourselves to him in glad and *willing* obedience. We see the Bible now as a record of his divine purpose that we, the children he parented, should grow in grace until we mature into the "fullness of Christ" and become capable of true sonship to God and fellowship with him.

We see in his Word his plan for the redemption and salvation of mankind, his long preparation through the ages for his incarnation in Jesus Christ, and, when the fullness of time had come, his entrance into human history through the babe of Bethlehem. Then as we study the life and teachings of Jesus and the stories of his death and resurrection, we come to know God as Jesus knew him, not as a far-removed omnipotent Creator, but as a loving, omnipresent, always-available Father. In John we read: "As many as received him [Jesus], to them gave he power to become the sons of God, even to them that believe on his name" (John 1:12).

One further element is essential in *Christian* faith. When the disciples were praying together in the upper room on the day of Pentecost, they were, as Jesus had promised, endued with power—God's own power—through the baptism by fire, the gift of the Holy Spirit. Samuel M. Shoemaker said of this experience:

These people were caught up and were living in a stream of power. I doubt if most of them could have given us a coherent account of who the Holy Spirit is, theologically, but they knew Him as an experience. . . . Not theory but experience—not explanation, but living power.[2]

This experience was not an isolated instance that happened once and for all. It is available to believers today, but only when we have entered into the genuine relationship of children to the Father. Only then is it safe for us to be entrusted with divine power.

Belief in Father, Son, and Holy Spirit—the one, triune God —to whom our spirits lift in praise and adoration and to whom, through faith, we lift our prayers, fully assured that he hears and answers—this is the essence of the Christian faith.

If this is not your faith but you deeply wish it were, then the

invitation is still open—"O taste and see that the Lord is good."
The promises in God's Word have never been rescinded:

Ask, and it shall be given you; seek, and ye shall find; knock, and
it shall be opened unto you:
For every one that asketh receiveth; and he that seeketh findeth;
and to him that knocketh it shall be opened (Matt. 7:7–8).

Draw nigh to God, and he will draw nigh to you (James 4:8).

Ye shall seek me, and find me, when ye shall search for me with
all your heart. And I will be found of you, saith the Lord (Jer.
29:13–14).

The promises of God are sure; he is faithful. The way to a
sure and saving faith is clearly marked. The signposts are
"Pray" and "Study God's Word," remembering Paul's teaching
that "belief, you see, can only come from hearing the message,
and the message is the word of Christ" (Rom. 10:17, Phillips).

6

Legacy of Joy

As parents we are concerned with the legacy we hope to leave our children. We struggle for years, sometimes depriving ourselves and the children of much that could make life a thing of beauty and significance, in order to amass enough money to try to provide *financial security*. We are fully aware of the importance of providing a legacy of *education*. We are equally alert to the need for a legacy of good *physical health* and for a cultural legacy of *acceptable manners and social graces*. But we seldom realize that over and above all these important things, far more fundamental to the child's future well-being, basic to his mental health and to his ability to function at his optimal potential as an adult, is his day-by-day, hour-by-hour experience of *joy!*

The happy child grows up strong enough to cope with the inevitable trials and tragedies of life. The happy child, secure in the knowledge of being loved, can reach out with love to others.

A child experiences joy most frequently from parents who are joyous. True joy is as contagious as chicken pox. And true joyousness comes only and inevitably from a religious experience which enables the believer to discern (even though dimly) purpose and meaning in life, in spite of all the contradictory and seemingly irrational elements. For almost two thousand

51

years the Christian faith has proved for countless individuals the rock foundation for such a joyous life-orientation.

The prophet Joel painted a lugubrious picture of a land whose inhabitants had forgotten the Lord their God:

Tell ye your children of it, and let your children tell their children, and their children another generation.

That which the palmerworm hath left hath the locust eaten; and that which the locust hath left hath the cankerworm eaten; and that which the cankerworm hath left hath the caterpiller eaten. . . .

The vine is dried up, and the fig tree languisheth; the pomegranate tree, the palm tree also, and the apple tree, even all the trees of the field, are withered: because joy is withered away from the sons of men (Joel 1:3–4, 12).

"Joy is withered away from the sons of men." Truly these words apply to our land today! Feverishly, men pursue the struggle for material possessions! Recklessly, people seek personal freedom and happiness in sexual license, trial marriages, and easy divorce! Determinedly, they seek to escape the consequences of their acts through legalized abortion! Satan-worship and unwholesome interest in the occult flourish amongst us!

In spite of all this, Christians have found the secret of the joy of the Lord. Far back in my childhood memories is a vivid picture of the first minister I ever knew, Dr. Howard S. Bliss, later president of the American University at Beirut. I cannot remember any word he ever preached, but I can still see him as he stopped to greet me one day as I was skipping along the sidewalk in front of my home. He was a tall man, and he had to stoop down to reach my hand. His face, radiant with joy and focused love, is distinct in my mind as is the sudden uprush of responsive love and joy that flooded my heart.

A legacy of joy is the priceless heritage Christian parents may hand on to their children. No other way of believing and of living can rival the Christian faith in sheer joyousness. Jesus said: "As the Father hath loved me, so have I loved you: continue ye in my love. . . . These thing＊ have I spoken unto you, that my joy might remain in you, and that your joy might be full" (John 15:9, 11).

Christians know the joy of their salvation. "For the Son of man is come to seek and to save that which was lost" (Luke 19:10). They have the joy of knowing the reality of the eternal life *now* and in the hereafter. "Behold, now is the accepted time; behold, now is the day of salvation" (2 Cor. 6:2). "Beloved, now are we the sons of God, and it doth not yet appear what we shall be" (1 John 3:2).

Christians have the joy of knowing: "The Lord thy God in the midst of thee is mighty; he will save, he will rejoice over thee with joy; he will rest in his love, he will joy over thee with singing" (Zeph. 3:17).

Christians rejoice because they know that true repentance brings forgiveness: "Though your sins be as scarlet, they shall be as white as snow; though they be red like crimson, they shall be as wool" (Isa. 1:18).

They know the joy of being used by God the Father to further his eternal purposes. They have found deep joy in following Paul's directive: "I beseech you . . . , brethren, by the mercies of God, that ye present your bodies a living sacrifice, holy, acceptable unto God, which is your reasonable service" (Rom. 12:1).

Pray that your children may receive from you their rightful Christian heritage of joy.

"The joy of the Lord is your strength" (Neh. 8:10).

"Thou hast put gladness in my heart" (Ps. 4:7).

"Be glad in the Lord, and rejoice, ye righteous: and shout for joy, all ye that are upright in heart" (Ps. 32:11).

"Let all those that put their trust in thee rejoice: let them ever shout for joy. . . . let them also that love thy name be joyful in thee" (Ps. 5:11).

"Thou will shew me the path of life: in thy presence is fulness of joy, at thy right hand there are pleasures for evermore" (Ps. 16:11).

"Enter thou into the joy of thy Lord" (Matt. 25:21).

7

Jesus' Redemptive Fellowship

It has been recognized that the one absolute requirement if we are to succeed in transforming our families into small redemptive fellowships through which we and our children may "grow in grace" is the recognized presence of the living spirit of Jesus as a member of the family fellowship.

This leads us directly into a study of that first redemptive fellowship of Jesus and his disciples. Jesus apparently lived with the little group with a twofold purpose: (1) to transform these frail, faulty, sinful men into staunch disciples who would so catch from him a basic relationship to God their Father that (2) they would be ready and able to move out from that intimate, blessed fellowship into the troubled world around them, "as sheep in the midst of wolves," to minister to the needs of people. (The existence of the Christian church today is a witness to the soundness of Jesus' chosen method.)

Surely this suggests a parallel for the task of Christian parents. Nurturing the family is, first of all, for the benefit of family members, but it does not stop there. At the same time the manifold needs of each member of the family are being met, the Christian family, individually and collectively, is reaching out to human needs in countless ways.

The final outcome toward which Christian parents look is the time when each child will have grown to spiritual maturity,

will have discovered God's particular purpose for his or her
life, and will joyously seek and accept God's guidance at every
step as he or she strives to yield life to him.

Four Aspects of the Fellowship

As we study Jesus' life, four aspects of his ministry to his
disciples and to the people with whom he came in contact
stand out clearly. Each of the four is equally essential in the
ministry of parents to children.

1. Jesus came making *a joyous proclamation.* He proclaimed
the good news of God's true nature, of his love for each person,
and therefore of the importance of each individual. He proclaimed God's claim to the wholehearted, single-minded devo-
tion of his people and God's always available and unfailing
strength for triumphant living in spite of all life's difficulties
and tragedies. He proclaimed God's forgiving and redeeming
love even for sinful people.

2. Jesus ministered to the needs of men by the force of his
example, by powerful living, by deeds consistent with his spoken
words which were radiant and lucid and narrated graphic, unforgettable stories.

3. Jesus performed *a ministry of service,* a ministry invariably and instantly responsive to human need—physical, mental, or spiritual—wherever it was revealed, first, within the
small fellowship, but also in every other personal contact. This
was an important part of his teaching by example.

4. Jesus shared with all who would accept it a quality of life
permeated by worship. For him, worship was not an isolated
act, perfunctorily performed. Rather, it was the fiber of his life,
every thought, feeling, and act the result of continuous God-
awareness.

A Way of Life—Love

In attempting to follow the example of Jesus' fellowship, it
becomes clear that his method was not to follow a set of rules
as to what to do or what not to do. Rather, it was *a way of life,*
creative and liberating, permeated by the realization that every

person is a beloved child of the holy Father, a way of life lived in continuous awareness of God's holy presence. Looking once again at Jesus and his disciples, it is obvious that he "discipled" his small group by living with them day by day, and week by week, with such depth of understanding love and concern that he could say to them: "This is my commandment, That ye love one another, as I have loved you" (John 15:12).

A Way of Life—Forgiveness

Love is the absolute priority in the Christian family; forgiveness is a part of love. Every family, no matter how sincerely and prayerfully they strive with God's help to live in Christian love, will know frequently the distressing occasions when loving relationships have been ruptured, when irritation, anger, frustration, self-centeredness, jealousy, or any of the rest of Satan's army of evil spirits will have raised their ugly heads. Children will sometimes be stubborn and rebellious; parents will sometimes behave like stubborn and angry tyrants.

God's Word gives us guidance for these inevitable times of failure. Over and over again parents will need to teach the children, *by their own example,* the biblical method for healing broken relationships: "Confess your faults one to another, and pray one for another, that ye may be healed" (James 5:16).

Confession must be followed by forgiveness—genuine, warm, complete. God's kind of forgiveness includes forgetfulness.

For as the heaven is high above the earth, so great is his mercy toward them that fear him.

As far as the east is from the west, so far hath he removed our transgressions from us (Ps. 103:11–12).

I, even I, am he that blotteth out thy trangressions for mine own sake, and will not remember thy sins (Isa. 43:25).

Forgiveness was a lesson Peter (like many of us) found hard to learn. "Then came Peter to him, and said, Lord, how oft shall my brother sin against me, and I forgive him? till seven times?" Matt. 18:21).

Peter was asking for some "reasonable" limit on forgiveness. How well Jesus understood him! He must have smiled when he gave his answer: no limits! "Jesus saith unto him, I say not unto thee, Until seven times: but, Until seventy times seven" (Matt. 18:22).

Overcoming Tensions

Creating this kind of Christian family fellowship is a task of herculean proportions. No one who has ever lived in a growing family, who has felt the bone-weariness that results from the twenty-four-hour demands, who has been exposed to the conflicting tensions and the never-ceasing pressures can be guilty of underestimating the inherent difficulties.

The incessant labor, the pressures and tensions, however, exist as an integral part of family living. They must somehow be lived with and endured. The effort to deal with them *in a Christian framework* does not increase the difficulties! It does not impose an additional task. On the contrary, it is the only method that holds out any hope for successfully handling family living. The mere effort, although the result falls far short of its potential fruitfulness, lightens burdens, relaxes tensions, and irradiates the situation with at least occasional flickers of real joy and at best with a God-given joy and peace that is only temporarily disturbed by surface squalls. In this adventure of purposefully trying to build a Christian family fellowship, times of discouragement and despondency are inevitable. Someone has said (and who would deny it?), "There are no perfect parents." No one of us lives up to the best he or she knows. Each fails abysmally to live out his or her deep and sincere convictions.

Humanity owes a debt of gratitude to Paul for having seen and expressed so clearly this universal experience:

For that which I do I allow not: for what I would, that do I not; but what I hate, that do I. . . .
For I know that in me (that is, in my flesh,) dwelleth no good thing: for to will is present with me; but how to perform that which is good I find not.

For the good that I would I do not: but the evil which I would not, that I do (Rom. 7:15, 18–19).

This one thing I do, forgetting those things which are behind, and reaching forth unto those things which are before,
I press toward the mark for the prize of the high calling of God in Christ Jesus (Phil. 3:13–14).

"Forgetting what lies behind." Few parents have such great cause for depression as Paul had. How bitterly he must have regretted his persecution of the early Christians! He must have been haunted by memories of the dying Stephen! Humanity has benefited immeasurably because he did not wallow in self-denunciation but was able to forget the past!

Parents, too, need to forget "what lies behind." Recognition of wrongdoing, deep and sincere repentance, honest confession to the children as well as to God, are good for the soul. But when self-depreciation continues to the point of interfering with a courageous facing forward, it becomes unwholesome. The surest proof of true repentance is renewed determination and increased effort to do better.

Maintain the Spiritual Glow

The strength and vitality of spiritual living depend upon constant renewal. In order to "maintain the spiritual glow," no parent can afford to neglect the sources of courage and power that have proved their value for generations of struggling humanity: quiet times of prayer and meditation, frequent and sustained Bible study, participation in the corporate worship and sacraments of the church and in fellowship with the body of Christ.

These are more than pleasant additions to a busy life to be taken advantage of in occasional moments of comparative leisure. They are the very stuff of Christian living, the essential food without which the spiritual life dries up and expires. You cannot starve your spirit any more than your body without dire consequences. "Man shall not live by bread alone, but by every word of God" (Luke 4:4).

You cannot be a source of spiritual sustenance to your family unless your own spirit is being constantly renewed. The New Testament suggests two sources for this spiritual renewal:

But thou, when thou prayest, enter into thy closet, and when thou hast shut thy door, pray to thy Father which is in secret (Matt. 6:6).

Let us consider one another to provoke unto love and to good works: Not forsaking the assembling of ourselves together (Heb. 10:24–25).

8

Christian Discipling

Before we consider the four aspects of Jesus' ministry mentioned in the previous chapter, one area of parent-child relationships needs some clarification—parents' discipline of children.

Discipline or "Discipling"?

What is the first thing you think of when you hear the word *discipline?* Many parents, if they answer quickly and honestly, will probably say "spanking" or "punishment." That is an inadequate interpretation of the ·word. Try using the verbal form *discipling* instead of *discipline.* What a different feeling it gives you!

Discipling is the method by which Jesus taught and trained his disciples: the method of the small, redemptive fellowship; the New Testament method for gradually changing imperfect human beings into their highest potentials as children of God.

How does this apply to our families? Each family is already a small, close fellowship of imperfect human beings in need of discipling. Each family, *if it chooses,* can be a fellowship discipled by Jesus Christ himself in which every need of each member is fully met, in which all are striving to learn to live in ways pleasing to God. "Till we all come in the unity of the faith, and of the knowledge of the Son of God, unto a perfect man, unto the measure of the stature of the fulness of Christ" (Eph. 4:13).

Parental Authority and Responsibility

The Old Testament makes it clear that God has placed upon the father first, and upon the mother as his helpmeet, the responsibility and the authority for *discipling* their children. This responsibility is clearly spelled out in God's directives given to Moses and passed on by him to the children of Israel.

> Hear, O Israel: The Lord our God is one Lord:
> And thou shalt love the Lord thy God with all thine heart, and with all thy soul, and with all thy might.
> And these words, which I command thee this day, shall be in thine heart:
> And thou shalt teach them diligently unto thy children, and shalt talk of them when thou sittest in thine house, and when thou walkest by the way, and when thou liest down, and when thou risest up (Deut. 6:4–7).

Notice also, in the same chapter, recognition of the parents' responsibility to answer their children's questions:

> And when thy son asketh thee in time to come, saying, What mean the testimonies, and the statutes, and the judgments, which the Lord our God hath commanded you?
> Then thou shalt say unto thy son, We were Pharaoh's bondmen in Egypt; and the Lord brought us out of Egypt with a mighty hand:
> And the Lord shewed signs and wonders, great and sore, upon Egypt, upon Pharaoh, and upon all his household, before our eyes:
> And he brought us out from thence, that he might bring us in, to give us the land which he sware unto our fathers.
> And the Lord commanded us to do all these statutes, to fear the Lord our God, for our good always, that he might preserve us alive, as it is at this day.
> And it shall be our righteousness, if we observe to do all these commandments before the Lord our God, as he hath commanded us (Deut. 6:20–25).

Children still ask questions! Children still want to know why, and parents still have the responsibility of interpreting the faith they live by. Stated in modern terms, parents still need to find a better answer to a child's rebellious "But why can't I? Everybody else does!" than the frequent "You do it (or don't do it) because I say so!" Children need to be told and to understand: "We are trying to be a *Christian* family, and so we determine what we do, or what we don't do, by the teachings and example of Jesus as we understand these in God's Word to us."

Parental Love

The Old Testament assumes as a matter of course the love of parents for their children. "Like as a father pitieth his children, so the Lord pitieth them that fear him" (Ps. 103:13). Here is one of the early foreshadowings of the teaching about God that Jesus later "fulfilled" in his emphasis on God as the loving, forgiving, redeeming Father of all men.

Again the Old Testament says: "Can a woman forget her sucking child, that she should not have compassion on the son of her womb? yea, they may forget, yet will I not forget thee" (Isa. 49:15).

Many Hebrew parents must have echoed the words of the psalmist:

Lo, children are an heritage of the Lord: and the fruit of the womb is his reward.
As arrows are in the hand of a mighty man; so are children of the youth.
Happy is the man that hath his quiver full of them (Ps. 127:3–5).

Many a father must have joyfully have joined in singing:

Blessed is everyone that feareth the Lord; that walketh in his ways.
For thou shalt eat the labour of thine hands: happy shalt thou be, and it shall be well with thee.
Thy wife shall be as a fruitful vine by the sides of thine house: thy children like olive plants round about thy table.
Behold, that thus shall the man be blessed that feareth the Lord. . . .
Yea, thou shalt see thy children's children (Ps. 128:1–4, 6).

These are all positive and eternally valid teachings in the Old Testament that foreshadow Jesus' own teachings in this area of parent-child relationships.

Children in Old Testament Times

Other Old Testament teachings need to be understood against the primitive civilization of their time.

From very early times, mankind's treatment of children has a sorry history (nor is it anything to boast about today). In most primitive societies, parents' power over their offspring was absolute and unquestioned. The Old Testament law about the "rebellious son" may quite possibly have been an early attempt *to restrict* this parental power, to require some other judgment than the parents' before the death penalty could be imposed.

Frequent references to the practice of *child sacrifice* are scattered through Old Testament pages. The story of Abraham's willingness to sacrifice Isaac (Gen. 22:11–19) needs to be seen against the prevalence of this practice. God used Abraham's willingness to give even this son of his old age to God to reveal that the God of Israel *did not demand or desire* child sacrifice.

This truth was made explicit when laws were finally written down: "And thou shalt not let any of thy seed pass through the fire to Molech" (Lev. 18:21; see also Deut. 18:10).

Child sacrifice (passing through the fire) was common among the worshipers of Molech. Through his prophets, Jeremiah and Ezekiel, God spoke against this practice:

The children of Israel and the children of Judah have only done evil before me from their youth: . . .
And they built the high places of Baal, which are in the valley of the son of Hinnom, to cause their sons and their daughters to pass throught the fire unto Molech; which I commanded them not, neither came it into my mind, that they should do this abomination, to cause Judah to sin (Jer. 32:30, 35).

Moreover thou hast taken thy sons and thy daughters, whom thou hast borne unto me, and these hast thou sacrificed unto them to be devoured. Is this of thy whoredoms a small matter,
That thou hast slain my children, and delivered them to cause them to pass through the fire for them? (Ezek. 16:20–21).

For when ye offer your gifts, when ye make your sons to pass through the fire, ye pollute yourselves with all your idols, even unto this day (Ezek. 20:31).

Old Testament Discipline

In spite of some foreshadowings of a deeper appreciation of and respect for children, in Old Testament times children were generally regarded as the property of their parents. They had no rights of their own. They were not considered of any importance at all.

The killing of the Hebrew boy babies in the time of Moses (Exod. 1:15–22), for example, is an illustration of the low value put upon children's lives. (Even in the days of Jesus, Herod slaughtered the innocents [see Matt. 2:16–18].)

We need to consider certain Old Testament directives against this background for considerable confusion seems to exist in the minds of many parents (and their counselors).

Certainly it is true that a number of Old Testament directives advise, clearly and positively, "the use of the rod" in disciplining children:

He that spareth his rod hateth his son: but he that loveth him chasteneth him betimes (Prov. 13:24).

Withhold not correction from the child: for if thou beatest him with the rod, he shall not die.
Thou shalt beat him with the rod, and shalt deliver his soul from hell (Prov. 23:13–14).

Thou shalt also consider in thine heart, that, as a man chasteneth his son, so the Lord thy God chasteneth thee (Deut. 8:5).

The rod and reproof give wisdom: but a child left to himself bringeth his mother to shame (Prov. 29:15).

Chasten thy son while there is hope, and let not thy soul spare for his crying (Prov. 19:18).

In light of these Old Testament directives, many speakers and writers today recommend the use of physical punishment

as a biblical directive. In fact, one writer, in an otherwise excellent book, goes so far as to say: "The Scriptural method of
discipline is clear and unequivocal: *the rod.*" [1]

I believe this is a mistaken and completely false interpretation of the Word of God; it is one more instance in which we
need to say, reverently and prayerfully, "We have read in the
Old Testament . . . , but Jesus teaches . . ."

In essence I agree completely that children require firm,
consistent, God-directed discipline for their wholesome matur-
ing. I am not recommending indifferent or lazy "permissive-
ness" on the part of parents. My disagreement comes with equating
"discipline" with the "rod." I believe the New Testament shows us
"a more excellent way."

(Incidentally, it is interesting to note that the "rod," so often
mentioned as a part of the shepherd's equipment, was used to
beat off the enemies of the flock, never to beat the sheep when
they went astray. That is why the rod could be a "comfort"
[see Ps. 23:4].)

Every writer I have read who recommends that parents use
the "rod" does recognize certain inherent dangers in this method
of control *if it is unwisely used.* Several are uncomfortably
aware of the appalling, steadily mounting statistics of the number of "battered children" whose parents obviously *did* use the
method unwisely! Much advice has been given on when and
when not to spank, on how to avoid unfavorable aftereffects,
on the need for reestablishing loving relationships that have
been broken! And yet, amazingly, one obvious truth seems to
have been overlooked by many advisers: Surely the best way
to avoid these evil aftereffects is totally to eliminate the cause
and to substitute other methods of control which do not entail
such dangers.

New Testament "Discipling"

It is against the background of lack of concern for children
as "persons" that was prevalent in the days Jesus lived on
earth that we seek to understand his attitude toward the small
ones.

In the familiar story of the mothers who brought their children to Jesus, the disciples were merely reflecting the current evaluation of children as of no importance:

And they brought young children to him, that he should touch them: and his disciples rebuked those that brought them.
But when Jesus saw it, he was much displeased, and said unto them, Suffer the little children to come unto me, and forbid them not: for of such is the kingdom of God (Mark 10:13–14).

And he took a child, and set him in the midst of them: and when he had taken him in his arms, he said unto them,
Whosoever shall receive one of such children in my name, receiveth me: and whosoever shall receive me, receiveth not me, but him that sent me (Mark 9:36–37).

And Jesus called a little child unto him, and set him in the midst of them,
And said, Verily I say unto you, Except ye . . . become as little children, ye shall not enter into the kingdom of heaven.
Whosoever therefore shall humble himself as this little child, the same is greatest in the kingdom of heaven.
And whoso shall receive one such little child in my name receiveth me.
But whoso shall offend one of these little ones which believe in me, it were better for him that a millstone were hanged about his neck, and that he were drowned in the depth of the sea (Matt. 18:2–6).

And whosoever shall give to drink unto one of these little ones a cup of cold water only in the name of a disciple, verily I say unto you, he shall in no wise lose his reward (Matt. 10:42).

These references indicate the value Jesus set on children. His numerous miracles involving children are additional convincing evidence of his deep and loving concern: healing the nobleman's son (John 4:46–53); raising Jairus's daughter from the dead (Mark 5:22–24, 35–43); healing the daughter of the "woman of Canaan" (Matt. 15:22–28); healing the lunatic boy (Matt. 17:14–18).

All this proves beyond any question that to Jesus children were *people,* as important to God as their elders; so everything he had to say about interpersonal relationships applies to adult-child relationships also.

All Jesus' teaching rests on and is an amplification of his "two commandments":

Then one of them, which was a lawyer, asked him a question, tempting him, and saying,
Master, which is the great commandment in the law?
Jesus said unto him, Thou shalt love the Lord thy God with all thy heart, and with all thy soul, and with all thy mind.
This is the first and great commandment.
And the second is like unto it, Thou shalt love thy neighbour as thyself (Matt. 22:35–39).

Jesus further amplified the meaning of *neighbor* in his unforgettable parable of the Good Samaritan (Luke 10:30–37) as "anyone in need."

"Anyone in need" certainly includes children! Every newborn baby is in need of one absolute essential if he is to survive. It has been scientifically established that newborn babies, given adequate physical care *but no love,* eventually sicken and die. Nor is love any less essential for normal development in the early years of childhood (or for that matter, at any stage of our existence).

9

Examples of Christian Discipling

The importance of love as the essential element in Christian discipling has been pointed out. *With love* it is possible to use even unwise methods of discipline without tragic results; without love no skillful use of good techniques will produce the desired results in children.

Often a single true-life situation is more helpful than many paragraphs of exhortation. Gathered below, from several different sources, are a number of true instances in which parents have used distinctively Christian methods in discipling their children. My hope is that each reader, in following with sympathetic imagination the incidents here described, will be blessed (as I have been) with new understandings and insights, with fresh belief in the power of love, and with a glad reassurance of the resources available to each of us as we reach out to avail ourselves of the unfailing promises of God for wisdom, guidance, and strength.

I DON'T LIKE PAUL

Peter was in kindergarten. Usually he was a friendly, outgoing child, but the time came when his mother became aware that Peter was making frequent unpleasant remarks about Paul. "I don't like Paul." "Paul's a nuisance. I wish he didn't come to kindergarten." And occasionally there were even stronger expressions, "I *hate* Paul!"

Things came to a climax when plans were begun for Peter's birthday party. "We'll ask all the boys in your class," suggested Mother.

"All except Paul," said Peter, decidedly.

Mother remonstrated gently. "We couldn't leave out just one boy," she said. "That wouldn't be friendly."

"Then I don't want a party," said Peter.

Mother decided it was time to investigate. She visited the kindergarten and found a distracted teacher struggling, so far unsuccessfully, with a situation in which Paul, a newcomer and a most unattractive little boy, was being definitely rejected by the group. Mother found out also enough about Paul to understand some of the reasons in back of his unloveableness.

At home Mother chose a quiet time for a long talk with Peter. First she told him a story about himself—how she and his father had been so happy when he came; how dearly they had loved him; and later how the three of them had rejoiced when little Dorothy was born; and how blessed they all were to have each other, and to be such a loving family. She talked about how carefully they had chosen a place to live that would be near a fine school, and how glad they were when he, Peter, found so many friends and had such a happy time there. To all of this, Peter responded warmly.

"Now I want to tell you another story," said Mother. "Not such a happy story this time." And in carefully chosen phrases she told of another boy, who through no fault of his own had never been a part of a happy family, who now had no father or mother or little sister to love him; a boy who had recently come to live with his grandmother, who was trying to love him enough to make up for the parents he didn't have. She said the grandmother had so hoped he would have a happy time in school. But somehow things had not gone right. He had not made friends. The other boys did not like him. They would not let him play with them, and so he was often angry and did mean things to the boys, and of course, that just made things worse.

"That's too bad," said Peter, his face serious.

"Yes," said his mother. "It's not a happy story. But I've told it to you because I think perhaps you could help it to have a happy ending."

"Me?" said Peter, opening his eyes wide.

Mother nodded. "You see, you know this boy," she said.

Peter shook his head. "I don't know him," he said, positively.

"His name is Paul," said Mother.

"Oh!" said Peter.

This was a wise mother. She knew when to stop. She had planted a seed; it would take time for it to grow.

Some three weeks later Mother visited the kindergarten. She had barely got inside the door before the teacher drew her to one side.

"I've so wanted to see you!" she said. "Tell me, did you say any-thing to Peter about Paul?" Mother admitted that she had.

"I knew it!" exclaimed the teacher. "Why—it's a miracle! He has not only changed his own attitude; he's swung the whole group with him." And she went on to give a detailed account of how one small five-year-old had deliberately set out to show friendliness to an un-popular member of the group with truly astonishing results.

This is not the end of the story: it had a remarkable sequel a year later. Dorothy had been three years old when all the conversations about Paul took place. A year later she was in nursery school. One day the teacher commented to her mother, "You know, it's a funny thing, but all three of us teachers have noticed it and spoken about it. Dorothy seems to be deliberately befriending little Mary. You know, she's the retarded child, quite unattractive, really, and most of the children shun her. But Dorothy is always going out of her way to help her."

At home Mother said to Dorothy, "I was glad to hear that you are being friendly to Mary in nursery school."

And amazingly, Dorothy answered, matter-of-factly, "Well, you know, she's another one like Paul—*she needs an awful lot of loving.*"

I REALLY WONDER!

A mother was trying earnestly to answer her six-year-old daughter's questions about God, when her fourteen-year-old son broke in, almost defiantly, "Sometimes I wonder whether there *is* any God!"

The mother paused only a moment. Then she said quietly, "But of course you wonder. Everyone does. You'd be a very stupid person if you didn't. People have been wondering about God ever since the first people lived on earth and discovered that they had minds with which to think."

The right to doubt and question! No true and satisfying faith was ever achieved without honest doubt. Children's doubts and questions need recognition and encouragement. When children are told, "It's wrong to question—you must just have faith!" surely they are not being taught to love God with all their minds.

One of the most vivid recollections of my childhood that has re-mained with me through the years, is of a certain Sunday morning. I was a little girl, perhaps twelve years old. I was sitting in our family pew at a regular Sunday morning service. Our minister was out of town that day and a stranger was preaching.

"Don't be afraid to ask questions!" he said, emphatically in the middle of his sermon. "The Christian religion is not afraid of ques-tions. The truth is never afraid!"

And my twelve-year-old self was caught up in a moment close to
ecstasy. I remember I pushed back in the pew and lifted my head with
a joyous sense of release, a sudden breath-taking conviction that it was
true! It must be all right to question, to seek explanations and understandings. The truth is never afraid!

That visiting minister never knew that a casual remark of his had
resulted in a deeply moving, never-to-be-forgotten experience for a
little girl sitting in a back pew of the church—an experience that
would remain a vivid, shining memory after more than half a century
of crowded living.

I'm Sorry

We learn by doing—an obvious truth, but one the implica-
tions of which we often fail to recognize.

A child learns to play the piano by playing the piano. Skillful guidance is helpful, and so is hearing good music, but no
child learns to play without manipulating the keys.

A boy learns to play baseball, obviously, by playing baseball.
Only as he plays does he gain control of his muscles, coordinate
eye and hand, grow in his ability to be a team member.

The same principle applies to persons striving to learn to live
in Christian ways. Skill comes only as Christian ways of living
are persistently followed day after day. And in this very truth
lies one of the great difficulties of the parents' task. To live in
Christian ways always involves not acts alone but the motives
and feelings behind the acts. A child may be coerced into doing
certain things, but motives and feelings cannot be coerced.

"Tell grandma you are sorry you were so rude," demands
a well-meaning parent.

And a still angry boy mumbles the magic formula "I'm
sorry."

Now sorrow at wrongdoing and wanting to be forgiven are
undeniably part of Christian living. Neither of these however
seems to have entered this boy's heart. To his original unloving
act of rudeness has now been added an untruth.

How much better to wait until the anger has subsided, until
a quiet time of talking things over may help him to be ready

to see both sides of the situation, to let "his better self" take over so that he may truly say a genuine "I love you" along with the "I'm sorry"!

FORSYTHIA TWIGS

Three-year-old Daniel in the very early springtime helped his mother gather bare brown twigs from the forsythia bush in the yard. He helped arrange them in a vase on a sunny window sill. He watched from day to day with intense interest as the brown buds swelled and finally burst open in golden flowers.

Sunday came. "I want to take some of the flowers to church school," said Daniel.

So his mother carefully drew out some of the blossoming twigs and gave them to him. At church Daniel trotted up the path and reached the door far ahead of his parents. On the steps of the church stood an elderly lady, a complete stranger to the boy.

"Oh," she exclaimed, noticing the flowers in the child's hand, "how lovely!"

Daniel's face broke into a radiant smile. "Would you like to have some?" he asked. And carefully separating a few of the twigs he held them up to her.

CHRISTMAS MORNING

Four-year-old Helen woke up one Christmas morning, and ignoring her gift-filled, bulging stocking, bounced into her mother's room. "Oh, Mommy!" she cried, fairly bursting with excitement, *"Now* may I give you the present I made for you?"

This and the preceding incident occurred in the same family. How had these two discovered the joy of giving? The answer is not far to seek. They had been a part of a loving family fellowship, where over and over again, they were provided with opportunities of planning happy surprises for those they loved. They were fortunate in having parents who could see behind the crude offerings of the children the love which they were trying to express, and who were able because of their genuine and deep understanding and appreciation to deepen the children's joy in the whole experience.

BETH—AND MARYANN

One day in seminary class I told my students about four-year-old Beth in India. She had cut the tablecloth, the curtains, and her hair, with her new kindergarten scissors. Then she waited to be spanked! Her mother had just been reading about the importance of being quiet before God, so she decided to try it on Beth. She suggested that they be real quiet before God and see what He would say to them. After some minutes mother asked Beth if she had heard anything. Beth answered, "Yes. Jesus told me not to cut the wrong thing with my scissors, and that you are to take them away until I learn to cut the right things."

One father in my class was sure this would never work with his children. That evening when he went home he found that his four-year-old Maryann had written all over the inside cover of an expensive new book. He saw that she was waiting for his reproof or punishment, so he decided to try the quiet way also. He suggested to Maryann that they be silent before God, to think about what God would say. Looking to God meant words to her so she started to pray aloud, but her daddy said, "No, this time we will not talk, we will listen." So they listened for a while. Then he asked if she heard anything. Maryann said, "God told me not to write in books, and to get an eraser and erase what I had scribbled in this one." [1]

DANNY

For two weeks I had the privilege of helping to care for Danny, an entrancing four-year-old. He had been an unusually cooperative child until his world turned topsy-turvy: his father died, his home was changed, and now his mother was ill. Most of the time he was his old sweet self, but by streaks he would suddenly come through the house like a cyclone, knocking down everything en route. His loved ones understood his insecurity; they did their best, but the tirades continued sporadically.

I felt sure the little fellow would have more security if behavior boundaries were set, and perhaps I had a better chance to set them since I was the unknown quantity in the household, even though he knew me well. So the first time I was the lone audience for a "cyclone," I quietly walked up to him, took hold of his arms firmly and looked him steadily in the eyes. He looked back expecting me to *do* something to him: but I kept steady hold of his arms and said, "Danny, when little boys act that way, I hold them like this until they get quiet inside." He did not struggle at all. After thinking for a moment, he said, "You can let go now. I won't do it again." I said, "That's fine," and let go. The next day he had to find out if I was consistent, so he started on a rampage again, with one eye on me. I walked slowly toward him as I had the day before. Before I reached him, he suddenly grabbed his arms himself and said, "You don't have to hold me, I can hold myself." And he did hold himself from then on. [2]

In *Heaven Help the Home!* Howard G. Hendricks has a list of "The Requisites of Christian Discipline" expressed in down-to-earth, practical, and untheological language but covering some important don't's and do's for parents who are determined that Christian love shall be the foundation rock of their discipline. The list is given here in abbreviated form:

There are two words I am always careful never to use—those words are "always" and "never." Let me suggest some things you ought always never use.

1. Don't use comparisons of one child with another. . . .
2. Don't make fun of a child—especially of his weaknesses. . . .
3. Don't use idle threats or bribes. . . .
4. Don't be afraid to say, No! . . .

Let's look at the positive side. What should we do?

1. Impart the expectation of obedience. . . .
2. . . . admit your mistakes. . . .
3. Allow the child to express his own viewpoint. . . .
4. Remember that discipline is a long-term process. . . .[3]

In this same book is the following bit having to do with "the first teen":

A Dallas mother of three girls . . . had been struck by the sobering responsibility of having a teen-ager. One day she told her oldest daughter, "Darling, I just want you to know I've never been down this road before. You're the first teen I've ever had, and I'm sure I'm going to make some mistakes. But I want you to know that I love you, and everything I do will be because I love you. If I discover I'm wrong, I'll be the first one to tell you." You'll never get a negative reaction from an approach like that.[4]

Blessing the Children

Larry Christenson, in *The Christian Family,* records this tender bit of family history:

A family in Germany shared with us their custom of blessing the children as they go to bed. The father placed his hands on the head of each child and said the benediction from the service of Evening Suffrages: "Our almighty and merciful Lord, Father, Son and Holy Spirit, bless you and keep you." We began to do this when our children were small—even before they could talk. I remember once forgetting to do it. Our little daughter began to jabber and carry on in a stream of baby sounds. When I stepped closer to the crib, she took hold of my hands, placed them firmly on her head, closed her eyes, and waited for the blessing. I knew then that this was no meaningless ritual. She was receiving something through that simple blessing. Is not this the very way that Jesus Himself chose to minister to children?*

"He . . . blessed them, laying his hands upon them" (Mark 10:16, RSV).

---

*Reprinted by permission from p. 163 of *The Christian Family* by Larry Christenson, published and copyright 1970, Bethany Fellowship, Inc., Minneapolis, Minnesota 55438.

The previous chapters have attempted to root our consideration of Christian family life today firmly in the Word of God.

The overall purpose suggested for parents is to transform their family into a truly Christ-centered fellowship, following the pattern of the original fellowship of Jesus with the twelve.

The difficulty of this task has been admitted; but no matter how far short of the goal we may fall, the direction of the effort is of primary importance.

Parents with the goal of a Christian family fellowship in mind will more quickly recognize inevitable lapses and failures. They will more readily seek and give forgiveness for intentional and unintentional hurts. They will more quickly and earnestly strive to reestablish loving relationships after disruptive quarrels and misunderstandings.

The child's Humpty Dumpty toy, that comic little figure which, as soon and as often as it is knocked down, springs back to an upright position, can be an encouraging reminder of our role as parents. Anger, fatigue, illness, selfishness, insensitivity, jealousy, anxiety, self-pity, and countless other human sins and weaknesses are constantly assaulting the fellowship we are striving to establish. The strains and stresses of family life can easily throw us off balance again and again; but the recognized goal of a loving, Christ-centered fellowship and a sturdy faith in God and in the power of his Holy Spirit at work within us can provide the force that pulls us back each time to our true selves.

PART TWO

THE PARENTS' RESPONSIBILITY

10

Proclaiming the Gospel

The responsibilities of parents in the Christian family fellowship parallel the four aspects of Jesus' ministry: proclaiming the gospel, teaching, fulfilling a ministry of service, and sharing a quality of life permeated by worship. This and the next few chapters will consider these four responsibilities in some detail.

Jesus' Proclamation

"Jesus came . . . preaching the gospel of the kingdom of God" (Mark 1:14). He made a proclamation. It consisted of the revelation of God's true nature and of God's claim upon his people. Understanding the proclamation and joyously accepting the claim are the underlying purposes of Christian nurture.

Two Agencies—Church and Home

The Christian church has always recognized its responsibility to proclaim the good news. The Christian family, on the other hand, with some notable exceptions, has spoken in recent years with a much less certain voice. Its proclamation has been feeble and unsure. "If the trumpet give an uncertain sound, who shall prepare himself to the battle?" (1 Cor. 14:8).

Our American civilization is suffering the tragic effects of the family's "uncertain sound" in the weakening of moral stand-ards, in sexual excesses, in juvenile delinquency, in corruption in high places, in increased mental illness, in racial conflict, in the unbelievable acceptance of abortion, and in the increase in crimes of violence.

The parent cannot avoid, even if he wishes to, making some kind of proclamation of life-values to the children. If it seems important that this framework of understanding be in terms of the Christian faith, the proclamation of God's nature, the pres-entation of God's claim on us of love and obedience cannot safely be left to the minister or the Sunday school teacher.

For more than a century, the church and its parents have been de-ceiving themselves. They have been living and laboring with the empty illusion that the Sunday School can and is doing the job of training their children in the fear and nurture of the Lord.

It's a lie most of us have accepted without question.

It was never a part of God's perfect plan for the church that an artificial agency handle the spiritual education of children. He has a plan. His plan is 4,000 years old. His plan when put into action works. Our poor substitutes for His plan have not worked well. . . . The facts are that our children are woefully lacking in both the content and practical application of God's truth.

God's plan is outlined in Deuteronomy 6:6–9. It lays the burden of teaching and training children where it belongs, in the home setting where it can be done most effectively and consistently.[1]

The Proclamation—Within the Home

"The greatest Gospel your child will ever know is not the Gospel according to Matthew, Mark, Luke or John, but the Gospel ac-cording to Father and Mother." [2]

This "Gospel according to Father and Mother" (whether Christian or secular) will usually be accepted unquestioningly by children in their early years. In the course of time, however, they will be exposed to many different points of view regard-ing the Christian faith and regarding the validity of *any* faith at all. Even in church school children frequently encounter con-flicting beliefs.

"Mom, our teacher said something in church school today

that I don't think you and dad would agree with," said an eleven-year-old boy at the dinner table one Sunday. And so began a long conversation about the parents' religious beliefs.

Not all children, unfortunately, bring their confusions and perplexities out into the open. Nor are all children clear enough in their own minds as to their parents' beliefs even to raise such questions.

In the struggle for selfhood, the need for independence may bring a denial of parents' ways of thinking and doing, a rejection of parents' gospel. Outside home the young person's faith may be rudely challenged. Few people go through college without having to give a reason for the faith that is in them, without coming into contact with agnostic and atheistic philosophies.

The chance of a child's faith standing firm through adolescence seems to be greater if all through his developing years he has been encouraged to search for honest answers to his thoughtful questions; if his opinions have been listened to and respected; if he has learned to listen to and respect differing opinions of others; if he has been helped to sense the limitations of human knowledge; and if his imagination has been stirred by the deep mysteries that challenge the hearts and minds of men.

Crises in Family Living

The time when a proclamation of the gospel has to be made, when some explanation of the meaning of life has to be given, is at the moment of crisis in family living. A father loses his job. A rainy day spoils a long-anticipated picnic. A child asks a question about a crippled friend. A member of the family or a friend is killed in an accident. Someone fails an important examination. The family moves to a new location. Newspapers and television report a major calamity—a flood, a tornado, an earthquake. A man like Dag Hammarskjøld is killed in a plane crash. John Kennedy is assassinated. Robert Kennedy and Martin Luther King die violent deaths. What day passes without some puzzling fact of life presenting itself for explanation?

What has Christianity to say about these and innumerable other situations? How, in a world with so much hate and suffering, can a parent proclaim to children a God of love? How present God's claim to integrity and obedience in a world where so often righteousness and "expediency" are unalterably opposed? How achieve for ourselves and for our children the clear-eyed unshakable faith that can face reality and still proclaim with Paul:

Who shall separate us from the love of Christ? shall tribulation, or distress, or persecution, or famine, or nakedness, or peril, or sword? . . .

Nay, in all these things we are more than conquerors through him that loved us.

For I am persuaded, that neither death, nor life, nor angels, nor principalities, nor powers, nor things present, nor things to come,

Nor height, nor depth, nor any other creature, shall be able to separate us from the love of God, which is in Christ Jesus our Lord (Rom. 8:35, 37–39).

The Child's Ability to Respond

The proclamation of God's love begins with *what we are* long before the child can understand words. Each child is equipped by God with the *ability to respond to love.*

How do we nurture the sensitive mechanism of a child's response? There is only one way to begin, and that is with ourselves. We, as parents . . . must clarify our own concepts of God's action in a human life and we must allow His love to operate through us to them. We misrepresent our Heavenly Father to our children when we lose faith in the power of His love which He revealed through Jesus, or when we hold in our own hearts a distorted view of this love. When we turn unwittingly to the methods of the world in forcing our own limited ways and thoughts upon the children, are we afraid that love won't work? Or is it that we don't know about love? God's love is tender beyond measure but never soft. It is stern but never hard. . . . God's kind of love develops and keeps open the natural response of a child to others, to life itself, and prepares him for his own life response to God.

When we let ourselves be irritated by children, this irritation reveals more about ourselves than about the children. Such irritations come because of love failure within ourselves and not from without by some act of the child, however disobedient he may seem. It is this lack of God-love in ourselves that closes doors in the lives of others— not only to us, but to life and to God Himself. His kind of love, God-love, *draws:* "I, if I be lifted up . . . will draw . . ." Jesus said. God-love *draws,* it never brow-beats. Jesus had faith in God-love. He did not force Himself on anyone, but they were drawn to Him, then and now.[3]

Rejected Love

One difficulty that stands in the way of accepting love as the rule for life lies in the fact, undeniable and tragic, that offered love is sometimes rudely rejected. Powerful as love is, over- coming at times almost insuperable obstacles, friendly over- tures are sometimes rebuked with coldness and good will is sometimes met with animosity; outreaching love sometimes en- counters malice and hatred.

This is harsh reality. The immature person, child or adult, reacts to an experience of this kind with anger and resentment. Usually self-pity flares up. "After all I've done for him!" It takes a high degree of maturity to recognize and accept the risk involved in loving and to hold fast to love in spite of possible rebuffs and rejections.

Even Christ's totally self-giving love met temporary defeat and is still rejected by many. The God-given freedom of each individual to accept or reject love carries with it inseparably the risk that the choice may be rejection.

Recognizing the risk involved, the parent who is trying to encourage his or her child to live by the law of love will stand ready to comfort and reassure when necessary. "Never mind, you tried. The important thing is to hold fast to love even now." These are wiser words than the more usual "Oh, forget it!" or "Well, if that's the way she feels about it, why should you worry?"

Recognizing the possibility of being hurt is no reason to give up the struggle to live and help children live in the way of Christian love as true "children of God."

The Proclamation—Beyond the Home

The proclamation of the faith of the family will surely reach out beyond the walls of the home. Social upheavals of our time demand a clear witness from Christian families. Only a family living alone on a desert island could avoid this responsibility.

What is your family's attitude on social drinking? on cigarette smoking? on the use of drugs? on integration in school, church, and neighborhood? on abortion? on capital punishment?

Christianity is relevant to these social issues and to many more. It has an answer to every problem life can present, and no family can remain neutral. The unconscious "proclamation" is inevitably either for or against the Christian point of view.

Christianity's answer is not easy or sentimental. It takes into full account all the obvious evil in the world, in ourselves, and in all human institutions. It does not evade the problem of suffering but staunchly maintains that pain, patiently accepted and nobly borne, mysteriously results in increased spiritual grace and exerts a redemptive influence on the sufferer and on mankind.

Christianity further proclaims that individual personality is precious in God's sight and that it is indestructible, destined for life throughout eternity.

Christianity dares to affirm that in spite of this war-torn world God is supreme, that love is ultimately the strongest force in the universe (not excepting the power of nuclear fission), that human relations are unalterably governed by moral law, and that most difficulties in which individuals and nations find themselves today are *proof* that such moral law exists and that it can be ignored or flouted only at the cost of dire consequences. It further proclaims (and this is perhaps its most unique and amazing contribution) that in the midst of sin and suffering and tragedy life can be lived, with God's help, triumphantly and joyously.

This is the proclamation parents must make the foundation for Christian family fellowship. It must be made repeatedly and consistently, year in and year out, in the midst of life. It must be the basis which sustains the family in the midst of crisis. It must be proclaimed and interpreted and demonstrated until its meaning illumines and transforms every day. "If the trumpet give an uncertain sound, who shall prepare himself to the battle?" (1 Cor. 14:8). "Lift up thy voice like a trumpet" (Isa. 58:1).

11

Teaching by Example

We turn now to the second aspect of parents' responsibility—teaching. Jesus proclaimed God's true nature and his love for every person by words, yes, but even more by the divine love within his own heart, by the force of his example. He lived with the twelve with such depth of understanding and concern that he could sum up all his teaching with these words: "This is my commandment, That ye love one another, as I have loved you" (John 15:12).

The Imitative Instinct

Parents too, whether they are aware of it or not, teach their children by what they are and what they do far more than by what they say. Most teaching occurs without conscious effort or intention on their part. Learning takes place as a result of the child's compulsive imitative instinct, a mighty aid. Praise the Lord that this is so! Take language as an example. We consider it an ordinary and quite-to-be-expected achievement that a two-and-a-half-year-old child, with almost no conscious help from us, has learned a language well enough to be able to communicate with those around him! This is a real miracle, as anyone who has ever attempted to learn a foreign language ought readily to admit.

A great deal of what we want to teach our children they

learn through imitation. Children who grow up in homes where ordinary courtesy is the usual pattern of behavior are very apt to learn to say *please, thank you,* and *excuse me* with a minimum of direct teaching. In households where correct English is spoken, children seldom have to be "taught" the proper word usage.

Language is not the only thing a child learns by imitation. In the Christian family, parents who are growing in their spiritual lives, who are interested students of the Bible, who have a genuine prayer life, who are seeking to discover and to walk in God's will, who are quick to acknowledge their own mistakes and sins and to ask forgiveness will discover that much desirable learning takes place with surprisingly little conscious effort on their part.

In an important and extremely helpful book, Dr. Thomas Gordon says:

> Parents, like many other adults with whom children will come in contact as they grow up, will be *models* for them. Parents are continually modeling for their offspring—demonstrating by their actions, even louder than by their words, what they value or believe.
>
> Parents *can* teach their values by actually living them. If they want their children to value honesty, parents must daily demonstrate their own honesty. If they want their children to value generosity, they must behave generously. If they want their children to adopt "Christian" values, they must behave like Christians themselves. This is the best way, perhaps, the *only* way, for parents to "teach" children their values.[1]

The imitative instinct in the child is undiscriminating. It works negatively as well as positively. We *wish* children would imitate only our good deeds and desirable behavior. However, our not-so-good ways are often more attention-getting because they are apt to be more dramatic. The only safe course for a parent to follow is always to be aware of both the positive and the negative elements in this continuous process of the child's self-education. When a parent is alert to the dangers, he or she will seek to avoid undesirable consequences of "lapses from grace" by being quick to confess to the children: "I was wrong. I should not have said [done] that! I'm sorry. That was not acting in the way Jesus taught."

Corporal Punishment?

The unconscious imitative drive in children is one reason corporal punishment, the infliction of pain to change a child's behavior, is basically unwise. Of course, "It works" (sometimes). The child may learn to alter his actions because of *fear* of the pain. (Fear of pain is one of the elements of cowardice.) Or the child may, if he is deeply rebellious, build up a stoic contempt for the pain, and the parent soon runs out of power! Besides, corporal punishment can only be a temporary method; you can't control teenagers by spanking.

In every application of corporal punishment, there is, moreover, a concomitant learning that inevitably takes place. The child probably could not put it in words, but the learning occurs. It is: "My parent [father or mother], the one who is supposed to be my model and my example in everything, deliberately hurts me when I do something he doesn't like."

The result of this hidden, unintended learning is that when another child does something to your child that *he* doesn't like he now has an example of what to do—hit the offending child. The seed of violence has been planted in his heart.

Parents who want children to value non-violence in human relations [and surely that includes every Christian parent who is conscientiously trying to teach Jesus' way of life] will seem like hypocrites when they use physical punishment to "discipline." I recall a poignant cartoon depicting a father paddling his son over his knee, shouting, "I hope this teaches you not to go around hitting your baby brother." [2]

At least two areas in our American culture today bear witness to the tragic toll violence takes in a country nominally Christian. One is the acceptance of abortion. Here the child's very right to live is violently abrogated. The second is the epidemic growth of violent crimes, including an appalling increase

in the incidence of "battered children." This is not the place
to discuss these areas; the daily newspapers provide ample
evidence of their tragic reality.

In the conclusion of an extremely interesting chapter, "Parental Power: Necessary and Justified?" Dr. Gordon has these
thought-provoking comments:

> "Power corrupts and absolute power corrupts absolutely," wrote
> Lord Acton. And from Shelley, "Power, like a desolating pestilence,
> pollutes everything it touches." Edmund Burke maintained that "The
> greater the power, the more dangerous its abuse."
>
> The dangers of power, perceived by statesmen and poets alike, are
> still present. The use of power is seriously questioned today in relations
> between nations. World government with a world court may someday
> come to pass out of the necessity for mutual survival in the atomic
> age. The use of the power of whites over blacks is no longer con-
> sidered justified by the nation's highest court. . . .
>
> One of the last strongholds for the sanction of power in human re-
> lationships is in the home—in the parent-child relationship. . . . A
> similar pocket of resistance is in the schools—in the teacher-student
> relationship. . . .
>
> My own conviction is that as more people begin to understand
> power . . . more completely and accept its use as unethical, more
> parents will apply those understandings to adult-child relationships:
> will begin to feel that it is just as immoral in those relationships; and
> then will be forced to search for creative new non-power methods that
> all adults can use with children and youth. . . .
>
> It is difficult to understand how anyone can justify the use of power
> in child-raising, or in any human relationship in the face of what is
> known about power and its effects on others.[3]

12

Teaching by Words

The Importance of the Bible

The consideration of "teaching by words" in the family fellowship immediately suggests, of course, the responsibility of the parent to help children enter their religious heritage in the Bible. In the Christian fellowship the Bible rightfully holds a unique place.

It is the record of God's action in history: the long years of preparation, culminating in his revelation of himself in Christ Jesus, and the accounts of the beginnings of the Christian church. The Bible is the foundation for the family's living faith. The responsibility for teaching God's Word to children has been specifically placed upon parents.

New Testament Priority

Since we are transmitting the *Christian* faith, our starting point is the New Testament; when Old Testament materials are used, they are to be interpreted in light of the New. An interesting example of the way to judge Old Testament stories is revealed in the following true incident:

A group of nine-year-olds were studying about Moses. The story had been shortened and much of the Biblical narrative had been omitted. One morning, just as the group were settling down for the session, Arnold burst into the room.

"You know," he began, even before he had his coat off—"You know, Miss Johnson, you didn't tell us all of the story. You left out some of the most interesting part." And in a torrent of words, Arnold proceeded to fill in the gaps.

"And when Moses led the children of Israel out of Egypt," he declared finally, "they took a lot of the cattle of the Egyptians with them. And that was all right, because Moses knew they would need food and things when they got over into the wilderness." He paused for breath and the leader stalled for time to think.

"Arnold has told us some more of the story," she said. "And he is right in what he has told. When you read the whole story in the Bible, you'll find all this and more too." By this time she was ready to face some of the questions raised. "I was interested," she went on, "in what Arnold said about the Hebrews taking the cattle of the Egyptians. Arnold says he thinks that was perfectly all right. Let's talk about it." Her tone was noncommittal, expressing neither approval nor disapproval.

"Oh, sure," said one boy easily. "That was all right. Why, look how Pharaoh had been treating the Hebrews!"

"Yes," broke in another. "Look at how he'd made slaves of them. And put men with whips to watch them."

"And made them make bricks without giving them straw," added a third.

The leader nodded. "Yes, that's all true," she said. "He had treated them shamefully."

"And Moses knew," broke in Arnold, "that when he got the people into the wilderness, they'd starve to death if they didn't take food with them." The leader nodded again. The group seemed in perfect agreement.

Suddenly Daniel stood up. "Miss Johnson," he said, slowly and hesitantly, "you know, I've been thinking—I don't believe Jesus would have said that was the right thing to do."

The leader took a moment to be sure her voice was still noncommittal. "Don't you, Daniel?" she asked then. "Why not?"

The boy just looked at her, frowning. "I don't know exactly," he said. "But I just don't think he would."

The leader turned to the group. "Daniel says," she repeated quietly, "that he does not think that Jesus would have said that was the right thing to do. How about it?"

There followed a moment of deep and thoughtful silence. The leader waited.

"I guess he's right," admitted one boy, reluctantly. "You know, Jesus said it didn't matter what anyone did to you, you had to do the right thing anyhow."

"Return good for evil," said another, suddenly.

"It really was stealing," admitted a third.

"And Jesus said, 'Do good to those who hate you,' " volunteered another. There was no dissenting voice.[1]

These children were judging Old Testament stories in light of their knowledge of Jesus.

A Word of Caution

Our concern as parents is not primarily to give children a *knowledge* of the Bible; it is to establish a relationship with God through his Word and with Jesus Christ, his Son, and with the indwelling Holy Spirit.

Only as their experiences with the Bible are rich and satisfying will this purpose be achieved. Parents must resist the temptation to quote the Bible *at* children in those distressing times when the loving fellowship of the home has been temporarily disrupted by flaring tempers or sour dispositions. It is true that Bible teachings are definitely relevant to such situations; it is also true that implied condemnation of actions in a Bible quotation will probably do little to help at the particular moment. These are times for parents *to quote the Bible to themselves,* not to the children; to hold fast to the love that "suffereth long, and is kind; . . . is not easily provoked, . . . beareth all things, believeth all things, hopeth all things, endureth all things" (1 Cor. 13:4–7).

The Need for Self-Education

"Thy word is a lamp unto my feet, and a light unto my path" (Ps. 119:105). So sang the psalmist long ago, but the Bible cannot be a light to our daily living if it remains a closed book, gathering dust on a shelf.

Many parents today, unfortunately, are ignorant of the Bible and are at a loss to know how to avail themselves of its resources. The challenge of finding spiritual resources in the Bible and applying them to family living cannot be met by a casual, half-hearted effort. Parents can succeed in this endeavor only if they are willing to pay the price required. A continuous process of self-education demanding time, thought, and persistence is part of the price.

Several difficulties face the beginning Bible student. The sheer mass of material is formidable. Here in this one book are in reality sixty-six books, comprising practically all forms of literature: folklore, history, drama, biography, poetry, fiction, letters, sermons, philosophy. The bulk of this collection of writings is enough to dismay busy parents. How much more must it dismay children when they first reach out eager hands for this strange and bewildering book!

The format in which the Bible is usually printed is monotonous and uninteresting, with its closely spaced, double-column, fine-printed pages and its artificial divisions into chapters and verses. This is not easy reading for people today, accustomed as we are to taking our reading in predigested capsule doses.

A still more serious difficulty lies in the need for background information. These sixty-six books were written over a period of more than a thousand years. Each one was produced for a particular purpose, at a particular time in history. Most are far from being self-explanatory.

For these difficulties, however, help is readily available to the earnest student. As far as the mass of material is concerned, parents need to keep in mind their purpose—the discovery of spiritual resources for daily living. In light of this purpose, even a casual turning of the pages of the Bible will soon reveal that not all its many pages are of equal value. In the first dozen chapters, for instance, are two, Genesis 5 and 10, consisting almost entirely of "the generations of Adam" and the "generations of Noah." No one today need expect to find spiritual nourishment in these long lists of names!

Or turn a little farther on to the Book of Leviticus. Here you will find page after page, chapter after chapter, of the laws of the early Hebrews. These are interesting in their revelation of how these God-given laws controlled all the details of their lives. These pages make fascinating reading for their historic interest, but it is not to be expected that much will be found in them to sustain our spiritual life today.

In the study of the Bible much can be passed over quickly, but much will be found to be kept in the mind and pondered long and deeply. The pearls of Bible wisdom and inspiration, however, cannot even be discovered unless the search for them is undertaken.

Modern Translations

The difficulty of format and arrangement has been partially overcome in some modern translations and in some printings of the Bible in shortened form. In some of these, paragraphs have replaced verse arrangements, quotation marks have been used, and poetry has been indicated by line arrangement. Access to several translations and paraphrases will prove interesting and valuable.

New Testament

If you are a parent recognizing your need in this area of Bible knowledge, my own recommendation would be to purchase, first of all, *The Layman's Parallel New Testament*. This is published by Zondervan Publishing House, Grand Rapids, Michigan. Here in one volume, arranged in parallel columns, you find the complete text of four versions: King James, the Amplified New Testament, the Living New Testament, and the Revised Standard Version. This would be an excellent beginning for your personal Bible study.

Opportunities for group Bible study are available in almost any situation. Look for them in the church and community, and take advantage of them as they are offered.

The Child's Use of the Bible

The difficulties presented to children by the format of most Bibles become increasingly obvious when any one of the usual reading books for children is examined. Notice the large print, the wide margins, the small amount of printed matter on each page, the colorful illustrations. Now open the Bible. No child would be spontaneously attracted to the Bible in its usual format, nor would he be likely of his own accord to try to dig out from its pages the parts that can have value and meaning for him.

Many attempts have been made through the years to overcome the forbidding appearance of the Bible. Perhaps the earliest attempt to increase its attractiveness was to furnish illustrations. Unfortunately early artists selected as themes for their pictures the most lurid and dramatic episodes. They portrayed frightful devils with horns and tails. They delighted in scenes of violence and bloodshed. They vividly depicted bodies writhing in hell in the torment of perpetual flames.

In my long-ago childhood, the family custom of observing Sunday followed the social pattern of fairly rigid restrictions on children's activities. The use of all such toys as bicycles, tricycles, and skates was strictly forbidden. Reading, with some limitations, was permitted. Three fairly large, red-bound volumes, standing on a low shelf of the bookcase, were looked upon with favor. These were books of page-size biblical illustrations with brief sections of Scripture under each picture. I have a distinct recollection, dating back to the days before I could read, of sitting on the bottom step of the stairs beside my older sister, poring over these pictures with wide and wondering eyes.

Only one picture has remained in my conscious memory through the years, but that one is still vivid: a raging, swirling flood, an uprooted tree, one or two frightened animals swimming desperately, the only land visible a single point of rock projecting perhaps two feet above the water, and clinging to the rock with one hand a woman, her other hand upraised and holding above the flood a tiny baby. So vivid was the picture that every time I looked at it I expected to see the woman's hand slip off the rock and both mother and baby disappear beneath the angry waters. Inseparably connected with my horror at that picture was the knowledge that *God had sent the flood.*

Many attempts to illustrate the Bible have probably done more harm than good. In recent years a number of "Bible comics" (no less appropriate title could possibly have been found!) have erupted into print. Producers and buyers of these strip pictures justify them on the basis that here is an easy, painless way for children to become familiar with Bible stories. But what happens to children's understanding of the Bible as they pore over these cheap, lurid story sheets? Perhaps, acquaintance with a few Bible characters and incidents so portrayed is a high price to pay for the damage done to a child's sense of the uniqueness, the "specialness," of the Bible.

Fortunately, this is only one side of the picture. Over the years a good many people have recognized the need to present Bible material to children in a less forbidding and unattractive format. The result is the current availability of a number of books intended to introduce children to the Bible and provide background knowledge of life and customs in Bible times. The best of these are excellent, beautiful examples of the best in children's literature. Parents need, however, to choose discriminately.

These picture-story books, however, are not an end in themselves. They are preliminaries to using the Bible itself. Sooner or later the child will hold in his hands his very own "real" Bible and will be ready to begin his lifetime study of God's Word.

A number of church schools present each boy and girl with a Bible, often at the end of the third grade. Most children look forward to this gift and reach out eager hands for it. It is sad that so frequently there follows a sense of disappointment, for the children's first ventures in reading their own Bibles may prove to be completely frustrating.

Fortunate is the child who finds a parent ready to stand by and help with knowledge and insight, a parent who can clear away misunderstandings and let the true message of the Bible speak to a child's soul.

In preparation for this time, wise parents will provide them-

selves with a concordance (available in paperback) in order
to be prepared for the inevitable questions, Where does it say
. . . ? or Where is the story of . . . ?

In handling the Bible with boys and girls, it helps to recognize and admit that the Bible is not primarily written for children. It is obviously meant for adults. Not only is the format
forbidding; the content presents difficulties. No one can read
far in the Bible without coming upon abstruse and involved
passages, the meaning of which is uncertain even to scholars
who have spent years studying the Bible.

The fact, however, that the Bible is a book written for adults
may well be turned to good account in challenging the child's
interest. "Most of the books you read," a parent may say, "you
read once or twice, or even several times, but then you outgrow them and they don't interest you any more. But the Bible
is one book you'll come back to over and over again. Of course,
even right now, there are a few parts of it here and there that
you can read and enjoy. And as you grow older, you'll find more
and more in it to interest you and help you. This is one book
you'll never outgrow."

It is encouraging, moreover, that enthusiasm is as contagious
as measles! Boys and girls growing up in a home where good
music is enjoyed quite naturally develop an interest in good
music. A boy whose father likes to work with tools is eager to
share that grown-up interest. Small boys playing doctor or traf-
fic cop or bus driver, small girls playing mother or nurse or
teacher or ballet dancer, are all spontaneously trying to enter
and understand adult occupations and enthusiasms.

The conclusion is obvious. You want your children to be
interested in the Bible. The sure-fire method for developing
that interest is plain: *Let them know you are genuinely interested in it yourself.* Let them see you reading it. Let them know
when you attend an adult Bible class. Talk about Bible passages
used in church school and in the church service. Be ready to
help them find in the Bible any verses they mention. Help them
mark familiar passages or develop a series of bookmarks.

"Hide in your heart" certain Bible verses that have deep meaning for you; share them with the family at appropriate moments. Be alert to references to the Bible in modern literature, of which there are many, and for related magazine articles and news items. Even a small child's interest can be caught by unearthing buried cities.

"Hid in Mine Heart"

A frequent criticism leveled against church schools today is that children do little or no memorizing of Bible passages. All Bible lovers will agree that it is indeed deplorable when boys and girls grow to adulthood without having stored away in memory many of the superbly beautiful Bible passages that have been the spiritual food of generations.

Parents are completely right in feeling that there is great value here that should somehow be secured for children, but memorization also has its difficulties and dangers. If the process of memorizing is an irksome task, imposed without regard to the child's desire or interest, if in the midst of the process the child is resentful and bored, and if the child learns to dislike the very words he or she is repeating because they are associated with an unpleasant situation, it is hard to believe that the net result can be satisfactory. The parents' real aim is not accomplished.

On the other hand, if the child's own desire to memorize a passage is stimulated, if he or she shares with parents a deep appreciation of selected verses, and associates with the use of the words a warm and happy feeling of family fellowship then memorizing will probably be well and speedily accomplished.

Here, as in many other instances, the example of the parents can provide an effective stimulus. "Dad and mother have decided to learn these verses by heart. We like to think about them and say them to ourselves sometimes when we don't have the Bible in our hands. We're going to read them over aloud every day this week (at breakfast time? lunch? dinner? bedtime?) and then see if by Sunday we know them." Given a wise selection of verses and careful discussion of unfamiliar words or ideas, it will not be surprising if children learn the passage by heart before parents do!

As a beginning, it will be wise to limit the amount to two or three verses, perhaps Psalm 90:1–2 and Mark 12:28–31. Later parts of 1 Corinthians 13 would surely be included and selected verses from Matthew 5, 6, and 7. Frequent review and recall of memorized verses is essential if they are to become a permanent part of the heart's treasury. For our children we want more than superficial knowledge of the Bible. We want a growing familiarity with its contents, accompanied by increased understanding and a constantly deepening appreciation of the Bible as containing the revelation of God. We want this increasing knowledge, understanding, and appreciation *to make a difference* in the children's lives as they come to "know the Bible" in the only way it can be truly known— by testing its teachings in the workaday world of human living-together.[2]

Jesus . . . said, My doctrine is not mine, but his that sent me.
If any man will do his will, he shall know of the doctrine, whether it be of God, or whether I speak of myself (John 7:16–17).

13

Teaching by Words (continued)

Family Conversations

Important as it is to teach, prayerfully and purposefully, the Word of God in the family situation, no consideration of "teaching by words" can ignore the teaching that occurs steadily and continuously in the course of family conversations, unplanned, unexpected, and frequently inconvenient.

It is a little frightening to realize that as parents we are always teaching by every word we say, probably most effectively when we are least aware of it. The offhand comment, the overheard telephone conversation, the hasty, discourteous greeting to a salesman at the door—these are all part of our teaching.

How unbelievably difficult it is to discipline the tongue, to make hasty, casual comments consistent with our considered beliefs! The Bible describes our predicament in no uncertain terms:

For in many things we offend all. If any man offend not in word, the same is a perfect man, and able also to bridle the whole body.

Behold, we put bits in the horses' mouths, that they may obey us; and we turn about their whole body.

Behold also the ships, which though they be so great, and are driven of fierce winds, yet are they turned about with a very small helm, whithersoever the governor listeth.

Even so the tongue is a little member, and boasteth great things.
Behold, how great a matter a little fire kindleth!
And the tongue is a fire, a world of iniquity: so is the tongue among
our members, that it defileth the whole body, and setteth on fire the
course of nature; and it is set on fire of hell.
For every kind of beasts, and of birds, and of serpents, and of
things in the sea, is tamed, and hath been tamed of mankind:
But the tongue can no man tame; it is an unruly evil, full of deadly
poison.
Therewith bless we God, even the Father; and therewith curse we
men, which are made after the similitude of God.
Out of the same mouth proceedeth blessing and cursing. My
brethren, these things ought not so to be.
Doth a fountain send forth at the same place sweet water and
bitter?
Can the fig tree, my brethren, bear olive berries? either a vine, figs?
so can no fountain both yield salt water and fresh (James 3:2–12).

In the midst of difficult conversations, prayers from the Bible
may echo in the parent's mind: "Set a watch, O Lord, before
my mouth; keep the door of my lips" (Ps. 141:3). "Let the
words of my mouth . . . be acceptable in thy sight, O Lord, my
strength, and my redeemer" (Ps. 19:14).

If parents are to establish and maintain communication with
their children, it is essential they make themselves *available*
when the children are ready to talk. Why is it, I used to wonder wearily, that the youngsters always seem to pick the most
inopportune times to propound questions of tremendous importance—the inconceivable vastness of the universe, God's
creative power and his ways of working with people, right and
wrong, the deep mysteries of life, birth, and death, and eternity? What parent is wise enough, without God's help, to answer rightly the questions of a child? But the questions cannot
remain unanswered without endangering the important line of
communication between parent and child. And from the answers children receive, they are gradually broadening their
understanding of the world in which they live, developing attitudes toward other people, finding a way of handling disappointments, controversies and conflicts, and entering into their
Christian heritage—or failing to do so.

One area of possible danger in casual conversations needs

special consideration. Many a child's most persistent prejudices come as a direct result of conversations where un-Christian ideas are openly expressed or taken for granted.

Prejudices

How often, for instance, do we allow ourselves to slip into a derogatory remark about some individual simply because he or she belongs to a certain group? "Well, what can you expect of a ——?" Or "All ——s are like that!" Or "I never knew a —— yet who could be trusted." Or "Don't have anything to do with him. He's a ——."

It is a rare parent who is not occasionally guilty of this kind of carelessness, with the result that seeds of suspicion, antagonisms, and prejudices are planted and nurtured. When remarks of this kind have been made, the wise parent is always alert to the need for counteracting them.

"It's never safe to say *all!* We have to think of people as individuals if we want to be fair." Sometimes a true experience helps. "I know a number of ——s, and they're not like that at all."

Some parents like to remind children, "You know, there are people, many of them, who are prejudiced against *us*. They think all Americans are money-mad and drink too much and drive their cars too fast and treat people of other races badly. It's most unfair, isn't it? And it's just as unfair for us to decide that we dislike a whole group of people."

Jesus' parable of the Good Samaritan (Luke 10:30–37) is an excellent bit of Bible material to use in conversations dealing with group animosities. A parent may introduce it by saying: "You know the Jews and the Samaritans were enemies. They would have nothing to do with each other. They felt about each other just the way you seem to feel about the ——s. And Jesus was talking to *Jews*. And he chose to make the 'good neighbor' of his story a *Samaritan*. If Jesus were telling the story to us today, I wonder what kind of 'neighbor' he would choose? It isn't what group a man belongs to that's important. It's what kind of person he is."

Jokes

Another area of family conversations that needs careful watching is jokes. It is amazing how many jokes belittle some particular group of people and how viciously this "humor" promotes and feeds prejudices.

One lazy summer Saturday afternoon a family and some friends were lolling around in the backyard telling jokes. The mother was busy with mending and only half-listening to the conversation when she suddenly felt something not quite right and glanced up. She caught a look of dismay on Helen's face and realized the cause. One of the family had just told a joke about a representative of a certain group, and there, trying to look unself-conscious, was one of Helen's best friends, *a member of that particular group!*

"I'm thirsty!" declared the mother quickly. "Who wants to raid the icebox and find us something to drink?" The joke telling was successfully interrupted, but the incident was not closed. Later that afternoon when the guests had left, the mother found Helen in her room, dissolved in tears.

"Oh, mother!" she sobbed. "Wasn't it awful? I was so ashamed!"

The whole family talked it over. "Gosh, I'm sorry," said the one who had told the joke. "I never meant to hurt her. I like her a lot."

"It might have been any one of us," commented the mother. "We're all fond of telling jokes and we've never thought about this before."

"We'll have to be more careful and think about who's around next time," said one of the youngsters.

The father said, "I guess that's not enough. I guess what we have to do is just never tell any joke that might hurt anyone's feelings."

There was a silence. Then, "That's going to cut out an awful lot of jokes," said Ned thoughtfully.

"But dad's right," said Helen, somewhat comforted by the evident concern of the whole family, "or else we won't feel free to bring friends home any more."

And so a thoughtless joke started this family on a long process of self-education. They grew in awareness of the vicious prejudices that can be spread by laughter. They began to look at all jokes with a questioning eye. They listened to jokes with a new awareness and a new sensitivity.

"Now there's a joke that's safe," someone would exclaim as they were watching a TV program. Or (perhaps even oftener) *"That's* not one for the family to tell!"

Helen said one day, "I can see what's right to do about telling jokes myself, but it's harder to know what to do when someone else tells them."

"I know," said Dorothy. "That still bothers me too."

"If you laugh," went on Helen, "you're sort of approving of it. And if you say, 'I don't think that's funny,' you sound so self-righteous."

"Sometimes you don't have to say anything," said Dorothy. "You can just not laugh."

"I tried that once," said Helen, "and they thought I was dumb and started to explain it to me!"

Probably no family will ever find completely satisfactory answers to many of the questions raised about jokes, but raising questions may in itself be a mark of progress in the area of human brotherhood, and the effort to find answers can hardly fail to increase the family's ability to enter sympathetically into the feelings of others.

Guided Conversations

In addition to a steady awareness of the possible effects of thoughtless remarks, it is helpful to cultivate the habit of consciously applying Christian standards to personal, group, and national conduct. Innumerable family conversations may reflect the parents' efforts along these lines.

"You wouldn't like it if someone did that to you," says a parent, "so of course you may not do it to him."

Or "Of course you're feeling angry and hateful. It's hard not to feel resentful, but sometimes it helps to find out why the other person was so mean. I wonder if . . ."

Or "You know, something like this happened to me one time. I was so angry! But later I found out . . ."

Or even "I'm sorry. I didn't mean to sound so cross. I know when I'm cross at you it makes you be cross right back again, doesn't it? Let's start over and say what we have to say pleasantly."

Sometimes it will be a news item or a TV program that will start a conversation, and the parent may wish to comment, "I wonder if the course our country is following is truly Christian or whether it is really based on expediency."

Children exposed to the influence of Christian principles consistently applied in all kinds of situations will tend in time to make their own judgments and decisions accordingly.

14

The Ministry of Service

Jesus invariably responded to human need whenever it touched him. The story of his life recorded in the Gospels is a continuing tale of compassion at work. At the beginning of his ministry, in the synagogue at Nazareth, he chose to read these verses from Isaiah:

> The Spirit of the Lord is upon me, because he hath anointed me to preach the gospel to the poor; he hath sent me to heal the broken-hearted, to preach deliverance to the captives, and recovering of sight to the blind, to set at liberty them that are bruised,
> To preach the acceptable year of the Lord (Luke 4:18–19).

This is also the "charter" for the Christian family fellowship.

The Family's Ministry to One Another

The family's first responsibility is to its own members. Loving, thoughtful, day-by-day ministry to one another is the most distinctive mark of the redemptive fellowship. This ministry is not by any means the exclusive responsibility of the parents to the children. It begins, before the children are born, with the two-way, concerned relationship between husband and wife, each giving to the other the sustaining love and trust that are the essence of Christian marriage. As the family grows, this

ministry becomes a crisscross of relationships, from each one to
each of the others.

Even the baby in the home has a special brand of ministry
although at first it is completely unconscious—merely the mysterious response to love, one of the most inexplicable of life's
many mysteries. Who has not seen a weary father, burdened
by cares and anxieties, suddenly released from the heavy load
for a moment by a toddler's jubilant welcome, the uplifted
hands, the straining arms, the joyous "Daddy! Daddy! Daddy!"
Or what mother at the end of an exhausting day has not felt
well repaid for hours of labor, for broken rest, for bone-weariness, by a baby's loving, petal-soft hand patting her cheek?

Every family looking back over the years could recognize in
its own experience numerous instances of the ministry of its
members to one another. A husband out of a job, a mother
struggling under almost unbearable burdens, a child heart-
broken over the death of a pet, a young person facing a major
disappointment—these and countless other situations are the
times when family love and loyalty count the most.

Two lovely illustrations of this kind of ministry within the
family came to my attention some years ago, both from the
same family, a three-generation family in which Grandma, close
to ninety, had been bedridden for over a year, crippled with
arthritis.

One day teenaged Julia came downstairs from Grandma's
room where she had been reading out loud.

"It must be awful just to lie there all day long and *do nothing!*" she exclaimed. "My throat hurts," she added.

"I know," answered the mother. "Grandma's hearing has
been very bad the last few days."

"Isn't there *anything* she can do?" persisted Julia.

"I haven't been able to think of much," answered the mother.
"Even with earphones she can't understand the radio. She
can't see TV. She listens to music once in a while, and she turns
over the pages of a magazine, but I don't think she can see any
but the largest pictures. She does love to talk. Just sitting and
listening to her is about the kindest thing we can do, I guess."

A day or two later Julia came in with a package. "Look,"

she said. "I got a pair of large-size knitting needles and some heavy wool. I can knit without looking at the stitches. Maybe Grandma can learn too."

Julia's plan worked better than might have been expected. Fumblingly, Grandma's arthritic hands manipulated the needles. At night, after Grandma was settled, Julia would stealthily bring out the knitting bag, pick up the dropped stitches, reknit sometimes all Grandma had done.

"She'll never be able to do it," Julia decided sadly.

But her mother comforted her. "As long as she thinks she can, it's all right," she said. "Your plan has already accomplished what you wanted—it keeps her busy and helps pass the weary hours."

Some months later, the second incident occurred in the same family. This time it was the mother herself who was the recipient of the loving family ministry.

Like many elderly people, Grandma was usually restless during the night. Often the mother would be up three or four times between midnight and dawn. Then, just when the family was getting up, Grandma would settle down for her best sleep.

Christmas came. The house was full of the spicy fragrance of evergreens. On Christmas morning, the family gathered around grandma's bed to watch her open her presents. Grandma exclaimed with delight over each package and then, weary, settled back against her pillows for a rest while the family moved down to the living-room to open presents in front of the fire blazing on the hearth. When the last package under the tree had been opened, the father brought out one more.

"This is for you," he said, handing it to the mother.

With great curiosity, the mother unwrapped the box, opened it, and reached inside. A small pitcher and sugar bowl came first, then a cup and saucer, a plate, and an individual coffee pot. She looked up, puzzled. "They're very pretty," she said.

"Part of the present can't be wrapped up," explained her husband. "From now on, the family gets their own breakfast, and you get yours—in bed, when we're ready to leave the house."

The mother looked from her new breakfast set to the loving

faces of her family. "You don't know what that will mean!" she exclaimed fervently.

Speaking of this experience some years later, the mother commented, "Oh, the blessedness of these extra minutes of sleep each morning! Vaguely, I'd hear the alarm clock go off and feel my husband's quick move to shut it off. Then he'd tuck the covers around me and tiptoe out of the room to call the rest of the family. Oh, the indescribable luxury of not having to move! I'd sink back into deep, relaxed sleep. An indefinite time later the smell of coffee would penetrate my slumbers, and there would be one of the girls beside me with my tray set with my special breakfast dishes."

One final account of "within the family" ministry. Fourteen-year-old boys are often considered to be unfeeling, inconsiderate, and irresponsible. One mother reports differently. The father of the family was in the hospital, seriously ill. The mother and the three children sat around the dinner table, painfully aware of dad's empty chair. Four-year-old Mary finished her dinner and went skipping into the living room. She stood on tiptoe and reached up confidently to the corner of the mantel shelf where each evening dad was accustomed to tuck a package of bonbons or lollipops for an after-dinner treat.

"No candy?" asked Mary.

"No, dear, not tonight," said the mother absent-mindedly. Nothing more was said.

But the next afternoon the mother was in the living room when the older brother came in from school.

"Hi, mom," he said. "How's dad?"

"A little more comfortable today," replied his mother. And then, looking up, she saw that he had just placed on the mantel shelf a package of candies. Never again during the father's illness did Mary reach up in vain for her after-supper treat.

How humbly grateful each of us should be who knows firsthand the unspeakable blessing of family love! Surely we can never deserve the countless small ministries that we accept day after day from those in our home. Small tokens they may be, but Jesus himself said that even a cup of cold water given in the right spirit was important (Matt. 10:42; Mark 9:41).

The Wider Ministry

> And above all things have fervent charity among yourselves: . . .
> Use hospitality one to another without grudging.
> As every man hath received the gift, even so minister the same one
> to another, as good stewards of the manifold grace of God (1 Pet.
> 4:8–10).

What a challenge for a family striving to be Christian! What has "the manifold grace of God" provided in your family? Have you been given a living faith, good health, a comfortable home, a reasonably adequate income?

What about special "gifts" the members of the family have been given? Does someone have a lovely singing voice or skill and training as a pianist or a violinist or a guitarist? Is someone specially gifted in art?

Does someone have a special flair for handling babies? Or for communicating with teenagers? Or for establishing warm relationships with lonely elderly people?

Is someone an extra special cook? Is someone skilled in the use of tools? Does someone have a rare gift for making friends? Or of spreading warm cordiality through a group?

If all the family has and is could be seen as evidence of "the manifold grace of God," if every special gift could be similarly regarded, and if the family could consciously accept its responsibility as "stewards," what an indescribably rich and effective ministry a combined family could offer!

The family that is learning the ministry of serving *within* the home will inevitably find its ministry overflowing through many channels *outside* the home.

A new family moves into the neighborhood. Perhaps mother sends a fresh-baked cake for supper. A neighbor's child is sick. A boy next-door may run errands. A neighbor's child has an accident and is rushed to the hospital. Other children in the family need to be cared for. A death occurs in a neighbor's family. How precious at such times are the loving ministries of friends! A family of a minority group moves into a home nearby. What is a Christian family's responsibility toward them?

Wise parents include children in considering how to meet these frequently presented needs, and they watch for opportunities for children to share in the ministry. "This is what has happened. I wonder what our family can do to help."

The other side of the picture is also important. The development of appreciation for all that neighbors do for *us* needs to be cultivated. "Do you remember when we were in trouble, how glad we were for all the friends who rallied round?" One family has developed a delightful tradition as a part of their celebration of Thanksgiving each year. They send "We are thankful for you" cards and gifts to neighbors and friends for whom they feel especially grateful.

An Enlarged Family

One very precious ministry is open to some particularly blessed families in which both husband and wife are dedicated Christians, united in their desire to be used of God. Every community these days has its quota of young people estranged from their families, floundering on their own, trying to find their way in life. One thing that has proved a blessing to some of these lost ones is to be "adopted" for an indefinite time by a deeply concerned Christian family, eager to allow God's love through them to heal and redeem these young lives. If this speaks to your heart, your minister can probably put you in touch with some love-starved boy or girl needing just this kind of ministry.

15

Christian Stewardship of Money

The Romance of Stewardship

More than fifty years ago, Harry Emerson Fosdick made some thought-provoking comments on "the romance of stewardship":

> Once in an isolated settlement of the old world of slow communications, a man could hear of cruel need in the antipodes and could go home with nothing but sympathy to offer. Let no man in this modern world express sympathy with any need anywhere on earth unless he *means* it! The acid test can straightway be applied. For we can *do something*, no matter where the need may be. The agencies of human helpfulness now reach in an encompassing network over all the earth. The avenues are open down which our pennies, our dollars or our millions can walk together in an accumulating multitude to the succor of all mankind. Each of us can take some of his own nerve and sinew reduced in wages to the form of money, and through money, which is a naturalized citizen of all lands, and which speaks all languages, can be at work wherever the sun shines. It is a privilege which no one knew before our modern age. It is one of the miracles of science mastered by the spirit of service, that a man busy at his daily tasks at home can yet be preaching the Gospel in Alaska, healing the sick in Korea, teaching in the schools of Persia, feeding the hungry in India, and building a new civilization at the head waters of the Nile. Only a man who with generous, systematic stewardship is taking advantage of the new opportunities is fully abreast of his times.[1]

Today no home is so isolated as to escape confrontation by human need in many far-scattered places. Red Feather, Community Chest appeals, Red Cross catastrophe relief, drives for support of medical research and aid to the handicapped, and many more worthy causes are publicized through mailings, newspapers, magazines, radio, and TV.

The attitude of parents toward these appeals is obvious to children. Is all such mail dropped in the scrapbasket without being read? Is the TV turned off or ignored during such appeals? Are they ever seriously considered as a part of a family's "stewardship"? And if they are read, listened to, considered, and (some at least) responded to, are the children aware of this family ministry?

Planned Giving

"How can anyone possibly give to everything?" a parent may impatiently exclaim. "And besides, how can you tell the genuine appeal from the false racket?" Indiscriminate and unintelligent giving is never wise (although even this may be preferable to no giving at all!) *Planned giving* (planned when possible by the whole family) is prompted by the deep desire to respond to as many and as varied needs as possible. It grows out of the recognition that all that we have—our strength, our time, our special abilities, and our worldly wealth—is God's gift to us to be used under his direction to forward his eternal purposes. A family might well make their own, David's prayer at the time of the ingathering of gifts for the building of the temple:

Blessed be thou, Lord God of Israel our father, for ever and ever.
Thine, O Lord, is the greatness, and the power, and the glory, and the victory, and the majesty: for all that is in the heaven and in the earth is thine; thine is the kingdom, O Lord, and thou art exalted as head above all.
Both riches and honour come of thee, and thou reignest over all; and in thine hand is power and might; and in thine hand it is to make great, and to give strength unto all.
Now therefore, our God, we thank thee, and praise thy glorious

name. . . . for all things come of thee, and of thine own have we given thee (1 Chron. 29:10–14).

Training Children in Stewardship

The parents' responsibility in this area is not just to be good stewards themselves; it is also to train children to be good stewards. Here again it is the inner motives and feelings that are important. It is not enough (nor perhaps even wise) to insist that a child "give" a percentage of his allowance. The aim is warm-hearted response to human need and a recognition of God's total claim on us.

Fortunately this is one area where concerned parents find little difficulty. Normal, happy children almost always respond with warmth to any need presented to them. Frequently they are the ones who present the need to their parents!

Allen, a twelve-year-old, came home from school one day in a thoughtful mood. He fidgeted around the room, twiddled with the TV set, and finally flung himself into a chair.

"Mom," he said, "there's a picture on the bus—you know, one of the advertising cards. It says, 'Hunger hurts,' and it shows a hungry child with an empty cup."

His mother nodded. "I've seen it," she said gravely.

"Well," said the boy, "can I send a dollar of my allowance to them?"

"Of course," agreed his mother. "And I'll add another dollar to it."

For small children, giving makes most sense when it is closely related to the experiences of every day. A new coat replaces one that has been outgrown. The outgrown coat could make some child deeply grateful.

A new pair of shoes may be the occasion of a small donation to help buy shoes for some needy person. One family keeps a baby's shoe on the sideboard and each member of the family drops in a thank offering whenever new shoes are bought. When the shoe is filled, the money is given to a director of a nursery who always knows just where a new pair of shoes is needed.

A child is sick and recovers. A "thank offering" to a local or missionary hospital is appropriate and perhaps a gift toward medical research in the particular area of the child's illness. A very special gift from the family (a growing plant, perhaps) may be sent to some shut-in friend who will *not* get well again.

A child learns to read and is caught up with the excitement of this new achievement. Now he might well be introduced to some of the many organizations working to help blind people, providing "talking books," for instance, volumes of Braille, and so on.

The red and black star of the American Friends Service Committee is known the world over. This organization has a unique record for planning projects for children's giving with strong appeal. Every concerned family intent on meeting human needs should be familiar with the work of this group.

When a boy or girl receives his first Bible is an excellent time to introduce him to the work of the American Bible Society which has been instrumental in publishing parts of the Bible in some two thousand languages. The Bible-a-Month Club sponsored by this organization (whereby a gift of three dollars a month provides Scriptures for a different country each month) is an interesting way of sharing in its work. Each month a card on which is printed a portion of Scripture in the language used in the chosen country is sent to each donor. An excellent way, incidentally, to lead a child into a basic knowledge of geography!

The United Nations is in ill repute in some quarters because of its failure so far to solve all the apparently insoluble problems of international relations. It has, however, a number of achievements to its credit, one of which is the spectacular transformation of Halloween from a mere fun night of begging into a tremendous, cooperative enterprise to provide funds for ministry to hungry and sick children around the world. The amount collected each year runs into the millions. The United Nations International Children's Emergency Fund (UNICEF) deserves the enthusiastic support of all people of good will, and its work should most certainly be a subject of discussion and continuing support in church-related families.

The list could be indefinitely extended. Jesus responded to human needs of many kinds—physical, mental, emotional, and spiritual. Parents will be concerned to share with their children a similar many-sided response as "good stewards of the manifold grace of God."

Giving through the Church

All Christian families are part of the larger fellowship, the Christian church, and some of the regular and systematic giving will be channeled through the benevolent program of the local church.

Giving this regular weekly offering has been made more significant in some families by a simple home ritual of preparation at some convenient time, usually on Saturday night. At the selected time, one parent reminds the children of some of the needs the offering is designed to meet. Then the offering envelopes for the week are filled. The family reads or recites in unison an appropriate Bible verse such as the following:

Take ye from among you an offering unto the Lord: whosoever is of a willing heart, let him bring it, an offering of the Lord (Exod. 35:5).

As every man hath received the gift, even so minister the same one to another, as good stewards of the manifold grace of God (1 Pet. 4:10).

This would be a time for the family to pray together David's prayer in 1 Chronicles 29:10–14.

Not all church-related families accept their full responsibility for the financial support of the church. Too many are like the woman quoted by Margueritte Harmon Bro, "All I wants is to be a bencher with no compelments." [2]

"Benchers with no compelments" are what too many church members aim to be! Too many are content to sit back and receive whatever the church may offer, feeling free, of course, to criticize harshly everything that is attempted by those few with inconvenient "compelments" who do the work. But of course it is a strange fact, readily observable, that the vast spiritual resources of the church are available only to those who enter the fellowship with wholehearted commitment.

The family truly seeking to bear its share of responsibility for the work of the church will have plenty of "compelments." To be part of the body of Christ at work in the world is a daring challenge. It is also a richly rewarding adventure.

16

A Life Permeated by Worship

We have considered Jesus' proclamation, his ministry of teaching, his ministry of service, and the parallel responsibilities for Christian families today.

The fourth element of Jesus' total ministry to the needs of people was his sharing a quality of life marked by continual God-awareness. If the redemptive fellowship of the Christian family is to move toward an approximation of the original fellowship of Jesus and his disciples, it will be necessary once again to capture the God-consciousness that permeates and redeems everyday living.

A generation or two ago "family worship" was prevalent. Unfortunately, the idea of family worship came to have unpleasant connotations for many people. It often amounted to long and boring interludes in the exciting business of living, with the father or grandfather reading interminable chapters from the Bible, some of which were completely incomprehensible to small listeners, followed by equally lengthy prayers, before the final amen released the "captive audience" to more enjoyable occupations.

Few of today's young parents have any such memories. The suggestion of family worship is apt to be met by them with embarrassment and an initial resistance that seems sometimes to grow out of an unwillingness to pretend they are better than they are!

When I was a little girl, the home in which I lived was lighted by candles and oil lamps. I remember quite clearly one day when some large cartons were opened with much excitement and some new, hanging "Angle lamps" were unpacked and installed. These lamps hung from the ceiling and had three separate wicks fed from a single reservoir of oil. They were infinitely brighter than the lamps we had been using. In time these lamps, too, were replaced—this time by gas fixtures. Still later the gas fixtures were replaced by electric lights.

In turn we discarded candles, oil lamps, Angle lamps, and gas lights, but we did not throw away outmoded lights and grope around in the darkness. We replaced each one with something better.

The old type of family worship proved in many instances inadequate to the demands of modern living. It was discarded, perhaps wisely, *but what have you put in its place?* The purpose of family worship was to awaken and keep vivid a sense of God's reality and continual presence. It was to root the family living in eternal verities. How are you accomplishing this purpose today?

No single area of religious life needs such creative, adventurous exploring as that of worship in the family. Discard, if it seems wise to you, old forms and old semantics. Call it what you like. Use old forms or find and create new ones. But somehow, in the midst of your crowded family living, make room for and give priority to the purposeful cultivation of Christian values, which is the aim and the result of all true worship.

Awareness of God

At the heart of worship is *awareness of God*. Singing, studying the Word, and praying may or may not be worship. The one essential that determines whether or not worship takes place is whether or not there is any true awareness of God.

Andrew Murray says, "Our waiting on God can have no higher object than simply having His light shine on us, and in

us, and through us, all the day." [1] We are reminded of Jesus'
words in the sermon on the mount: "[*God*] maketh his sun to
rise on the evil and on the good" (Matt. 5:45).
Andrew Murray goes on:

God is light. God is a sun. Paul says: "God hath shined in our
hearts to give the light." What light? "The light of the glory of God,
in the face of Jesus Christ." Just as the sun shines its beautiful, life-
giving light on and into our earth, so God shines into our hearts the
light of His glory, of His love, in Christ His Son. Our heart is meant
to have light filling and gladdening it all the day. . . .
   But can we indeed enjoy it all the day? We can. And how can we?
Let nature give us the answer. Those beautiful trees and flowers, with
all this green grass, what do they do to keep the sun shining on them?
They do nothing; they simply bask in the sunshine, when it comes.
The sun is millions of miles away, but over all that distance it
comes, . . . and the tiniest flower that lifts its little head upward
is met by the same exuberance of light and blessing as flood the
widest landscape. . . .
   The only difference between nature and grace is this, that what the
trees and the flowers do unconsciously, as they drink in the blessing
of the light, is to be with us a voluntary and a loving acceptance.
Faith, simple faith in God's Word and love, is to be the opening of
the eyes, the opening of the heart, to receive and enjoy the unspeakable glory of His grace. And just as the trees, day by day, and month
by month, stand and grow into beauty and fruitfulness, just welcoming
whatever sunshine the sun may give, so it is the very highest exercise
of our Christian life just to abide in the light of God, and let it, and
let Him, fill us with the life and the brightness it brings.
   And if you ask, But can it really be, that just as naturally and
heartily as I recognize and rejoice in the beauty of a bright sunny
morning, I can rejoice in God's light all the day? It can, indeed. . . .
   Just bow even now, in stillness before God, and wait on Him to
shine into you. Say, in humble faith, God is light, infinitely brighter
and more beautiful than that of the sun. God is light—the Father. The
eternal, inaccessible, and incomprehensible light—the Son. The light
concentrated, and embodied, and manifested—the Spirit, the light
entering and dwelling and shining in our hearts. God is light, and is
here shining on my heart. . . . I will take time, and just be still, and
rest in the light of God. [2]

Parents who have experienced the abiding presence of God

will be ready to share this awareness in intimate moments of
family fellowship.

Times for Withdrawal

If we as parents are to grow in our spiritual understandings,
we need to strive earnestly for periods of withdrawal when we
can expose our hearts to the glory of God, when we can look
at our lives in the light of his truth, when we can remind ourselves of our life purposes and receive from him the clear sense
of his direction.

In this withdrawal we are clearly following the example of
our master Jesus: "And in the morning, rising up a great while
before day, he went out, and departed into a solitary place,
and there prayed" (Mark 1:35).

At the very beginning and again near the end of Jesus' public ministry there were similar withdrawals for prayer—the
forty days in the wilderness and the lonely vigil in Gethsemane.
Between these two are scattered incidents indicating that
prayer and meditation were an important part of his busy days.

That these habitual periods of withdrawal were fruitful, that
Jesus came back from them renewed and invigorated, was
clearly recognized by the disciples. "Lord, teach us to pray"
(Luke 11:1) one of them demanded one day. What an astonishing request, for the disciples were all Jews. From early childhood they had been trained in the frequent ritualistic repetition
of prayers. How doubly significant, therefore, was the demand
"Lord, teach us to pray"! What they weie really asking was
"Lord, teach us to pray *as you do,* so that we may channel into
our lives the infinite power of almighty God."

The "solitary place," the fenced-in corner of time and space
for quiet meditation and prayer, can never be achieved without effort. Every such period, no matter how brief, should begin with "waiting on the Lord" until a genuine awareness of
his presence is achieved.

In addition to our determination to achieve for ourselves
this habitual time for prayer, let us not fail to recognize also

the inestimable value of frequent mental withdrawals even in the midst of daily activities. Think for a moment of the hours often spent (and sometimes wasted) by fathers commuting to work or driving alone. Think of the hours mothers spend at countless physical tasks that keep their hands busy but leave their minds free. Here are "solitary places" ready to be used, waiting to be filled with the renewal of spiritual strength and power from the unseen but always available Source.

Isaiah's Call to Be a Prophet

Parents just beginning their practice of daily devotions may like to read the story of Isaiah's call to be a prophet for God (Isa. 6:1–8) and may pattern their prayers along the lines of his experience: (1) awareness of God, praise, and thanksgiving; (2) confession and repentance; (3) acceptance of God's forgiveness; and (4) rededication of all life to God's will and purpose.

The "Desperate Need" of Prayer

A good many years ago, Georgia Harkness wrote: "Of all the things the world now desperately needs, none is more needed than an upsurge of vital, God-centered, intelligently grounded prayer.[3] She followed this with a list of other much needed things—a new international order, control of atomic energy for constructive purposes, more understanding and justice between labor and management, the end of poverty and hunger, and so on. And then she reiterated her previous comment: "Nothing is more needed than a general upsurge of the right kind of prayer."

This is a thought-provoking statement, and some readers, I am sure, will question its validity. Tragically, to many people today, prayer is a lost art.

"It doesn't make sense," someone will say. "Even if you grant the existence of God, he isn't going to be coaxed into changing anything just because I ask him to. And besides, maybe someone else is praying to him for just the opposite thing! For example, in a war, when both sides are praying for victory. He can't possibly answer both prayers." (Are not *no, not yet,* and *later* also answers to prayer?)

Such comments reveal a woeful lack of understanding of "vital, God-centered, intelligently grounded prayer." Because the point of view expressed is still fairly prevalent, it may be helpful to state quite positively and simply what genuine prayer is *not.* It is not asking God for special favors or preferential treatment. It is not advising God or trying to dictate to him how to run his universe.

On the contrary, "God-centered prayer" is first of all an opening of the heart to God, a turning toward him in expectancy, a waiting for the welling-up of his Spirit within the heart, a tuning-in of the body, mind, and spirit in order to receive what God is ready to communicate.

As one approaches any moment of informal or formal prayer, one thought ought to be held firmly in the heart. It is not in reality we who are calling on God to answer us. The reverse is true: God has initiated the contact. He has called us, and we are answering his call: "Behold, I stand at the door, and knock: if any man hear my voice, and open the door, I will come in to him" (Rev. 3:20).

17

A Life Permeated by Worship (continued)

The previous chapter dealt in some detail with parents' prayer life. No parents can hope to guide their children's prayer experience unless they themselves are constantly and steadily growing in their ability to respond to God, "to wait on the Lord," and to know the reality of his presence.

This chapter will deal with prayer in the family, with a few specific practical suggestions about how parents may share with children their own search for a more continuous God-awareness in their daily lives.

A Daily Pattern for the Family

Four daily times for prayer are suggested: in the morning, at mealtimes, during the day, and in the evening. In each section some appropriate Bible verse prayers are suggested. The use of Bible prayers is not meant to be a substitute for the spontaneous outpourings of the parent's or child's own prayers. It is meant rather to stimulate and encourage such personal expressions by providing patterns and a rich language of worship. Merely to repeat these Bible verses is not, of course, necessarily *to pray*. As a person chooses the passages that truly express his own feelings and uses them as though they were being said for the first time with a genuine awareness of God, they will become prayer.

Prayer in the Morning

Those who have mastered the art of effective prayer stress the importance of centering the first waking thoughts on God. This need not be a long and extended period of prayer. A few seconds is enough to focus the heart on God and set the tone for the day's activities.

One device to help establish this quick uplift of the heart to God on first awaking is the use of "prayer cards." The family may choose together certain reminder prayer verses (see possibilities below), and these may be printed on cards, one for each member of the family. The cards may then be placed on a bedside table or on a bureau where they will serve as a reminder each morning. Cards about five by nine inches are a good size; fold in half so that they stand up like a tent; print a verse on each side; then fold inside out and add other verses.

Some fathers, skillful with tools, have made lovely holders for the cards (unfolded) from rough slabs of cedar wood, sometimes with the bark left on. And some mothers have "illuminated" the verses with touches of color and small illustrations or decorations.

It probably does not need to be pointed out that the example of the parent in using the cards, and in referring to them occasionally, will be a mighty stimulus to the child's use and a tremendous aid in establishing the habit of morning worship.

Use the same card until the words are firmly "hid in the heart" and add different verses from time to time.

Below are a few suggested verses for use in this way:

This is the day which thou, O Lord, hast made; we will rejoice and be glad in it (see Ps. 118:24).

Lord, thou hast been our dwelling place in all generations.
Before the mountains were brought forth, or ever thou hadst formed the earth and the world, even from everlasting to everlasting, thou art God (Ps. 90:1–2).

Teach me thy way, O Lord; I will walk in thy truth (Ps. 86:11).

Search me, O God, and know my heart: try me, and know my thoughts:

And see if there be any wicked way in me, and lead me in the way everlasting (Ps. 139:23–24).

Whither shall I go from thy spirit? or whither shall I flee from thy presence?

If I ascend up into heaven, thou art there: if I make my bed in hell, behold, thou art there.

If I take the wings of the morning, and dwell in the uttermost parts of the sea;

Even there shall thy hand lead me, and thy right hand shall hold me.

If I say, Surely the darkness shall cover me; even the night shall be light about me.

Yea, the darkness hideth not from thee; but the night shineth as the day: the darkness and the light are both alike to thee (Ps. 139:7–12).

Be on the lookout during your times of Bible study for passages which by the change of a word or two can become prayers (see Ps. 118:24 above). Verses, for instance in 1 Corinthians 13, seem perfectly designed to be "prayed" by every Christian family:

> Give us grace, O loving God,
>   to love with the love
>   that suffereth long,
>   and is kind;
>   that envieth not;
>   that vaunteth not itself;
>   is not puffed up;
>   that doth not behave itself unseemly;
>   seeketh not her own,
>   is not easily provoked,
>   thinketh no evil;
>   that rejoiceth not in iniquity,
>   but rejoiceth in the truth;
>   beareth all things,
>   believeth all things,
>   hopeth all things,
>   endureth all things;
>   the love that never faileth (see 1 Cor. 13:4–8).[1]

Prayer during the Day

In addition to the habit of morning prayer, each of us needs to cultivate the practice of lifting the heart to God frequently in the course of every day.

One way of accomplishing this is to train ourselves and our children to brief *flash memories* or *flash prayers* by choosing certain reminders of Jesus' teachings and always having a quick recall of his words whenever we touch, see, or hear these particular things.

Jesus used this method of making everyday things the symbols of his spiritual teachings:

Salt—Matthew 5:13
Light—Matthew 5:14
Birds—Matthew 6:26
Lilies—Matthew 6:28
Houses—Matthew 7:24–25
Sparrows—Matthew 10:29
Sun and rain—Matthew 5:45
Leaven—Matthew 13:33
Mustard seed—Matthew 13:31
Bread—John 6:35
Cup of cold water—Mark 9:41

So we today may keep alive in our hearts and minds some of Jesus' teachings by associating them persistently and repeatedly with everyday things around us. We can purposefully increase our awareness of the deep and eternal verities by using everyday things around us to be constant reminders of the values we are striving to incarnate in our family living.

The suggestions below are specifically for parents, but once parents have proved themselves the effectiveness of the use of "reminders" to keep themselves in continual awareness of God, they will be able naturally and easily to share this important technique with their children.

Suppose, for instance, that a mother trained herself to have a *flash memory* every time she picked up a salt cellar: "Ye are the salt of the earth" (Matt. 5:13). How could she fail to ask herself each time, "Is the flavor I am adding to the family life now, this minute, bringing out all that is good and wholesome?"

Suppose a father trained himself to have a *flash memory* every time he touched a light switch: "Ye are the light of the world" (Matt. 5:14). Could he fail to wonder, "Am I truly a light to my family? Is the home brighter, more cheerful, more truly Christian because I am here? Are the children really being enlightened by my words and by my actions? Or am I adding to their confusion?"

Suppose every time parents felt the warmth of the sun they had a *flash memory:* "Your Father . . . maketh his sun to rise on the evil and on the good" (Matt. 5:45). How could they fail to ask, "Is our love for each other, and for the children, like that—steady, dependable, life-giving?"

Suppose every time we saw sparrows we had a *flash memory:* "Are not five sparrows sold for two farthings, and not one of them is forgotten before God? . . . Fear not therefore: ye are of more value than many sparows" (Luke 12:6–7). Of value—to God! Would we not lift up our heads and straighten our shoulders and carry the daily load a bit more easily inspired by that thought?

Such moments are truly prayer moments though no words of prayer may be formulated.

Parents growing in their own prayer life will discover and use frequent opportunities to pray *with the children* particular *flash prayers* suggested by circumstances. Sometimes this will be a one-parent-one-child happening; sometimes it will be a whole-family time of prayer.

Individual prayers might be for a child facing an examination or a trip to the doctor's office or for a child who has been hurt, physically or emotionally, and is in need of healing. Family prayers might be when one member is going away to school or on a journey or when the family has learned of some emergency in a neighbor's family and is seeking guidance on how to minister. The list could be extended indefinitely. The opportunities are all around us. The parent needs to open his spiritual eyes to perceive them and then to overcome his initial reluctance or embarrassment so that for him and for the children prayer becomes a natural and important part of every day. No more effective way than this can be found to nurture the prayer life of each child.

Prayer at Mealtimes

The custom of grace at table has persisted in some homes where it is the only form of worship in which the family joins. Its inadequacies are obvious; it very easily degenerates into a meaningless routine that is uninspired and irreverent, *but this need not happen.*

One way to avoid this is to select and use some of the lovely Bible verses that adequately express the gratitude of the heart. It will be helpful if selected verses are typed or printed on cards. These verses may be used in a variety of ways. Children may take turns in choosing and repeating one; or a selected verse may be memorized and repeated in unison; or each member of the family may choose one and the verses may be read in turn.

Children often enjoy making up original tunes for the verses, and if their tunes are used, they enter into the grace with new understanding and enjoyment. Some musical families enjoy chanting one of the brief verses. This may even be done very simply in parts. The father may chant, for instance, "We give thanks unto thee, O God" (see Ps. 75:1), on the first note of the scale. The children may then chant the same words on the third note; the mother following on the fifth, and concluding with all singing together in harmony. This makes a really lovely and unusual grace.

One family with Quaker leanings varies the procedure by having a silent grace, with hands joined around the table.

A few appropriate Bible graces are given below. Watch for others as you read and study the Bible.

We give thanks unto thee, O Lord; for thou art good: for thy mercy endureth for ever (see Ps. 106:1).

I will praise thee, O Lord, with my whole heart; I will shew forth all thy marvellous works.

I will be glad and rejoice in thee: I will sing praise to thy name, O thou most High (Ps. 9:1–2).

It is a good thing to give thanks unto thee, O Lord, and to sing praises unto thy name, O most High:

To show forth thy lovingkindness in the morning, and thy faithfulness at night (see Ps. 92:1–2).

Thou, Lord, hast done great things for us; whereof we are glad (see Ps. 126:3).

O Lord, how manifold are thy works! in wisdom hast thou made them all: the earth is full of thy riches.

So is this great and wide sea, wherein are things creeping innumerable, both small and great beasts. . . .

These wait all upon thee; that thou mayest give them their meat in due season.

That thou givest them they gather: thou openest thine hand, they are filled with good (Ps. 104:24–28).

I will sing unto thee, O Lord, as long as I live: I will sing praise to thee, my God, while I have my being (see Ps. 104:33).

Prayer in the Evening

The beginning and the end of the day seem to be especially appropriate times for prayer. At night when the day's work is ended, a temptation sometimes comes to sink down into self-pity, to go over the disappointments and failures of the day, to brood over small hurts until they become exaggerated out of all proportion to their real significance. Then each of us needs to follow the psalmist's advice: "Bless the Lord, O my soul, and forget not all his benefits" (Ps. 103:2).

Concentrating our minds on things for which we are thankful will nearly always lift us above self-centered narrowness and pettiness. Moreover, counting our blessings is one sure way of increasing our appreciation for the love and forgiveness of Christian family living.

The evening prayer seems naturally to fall into three parts: thanksgiving, confession, and recommitment to what is highest and best. After these, it is comforting to put all thoughts out of the mind save a reassuring recollection of God's steadfast love!

The parent and the child who have memorized some of the great, inspired passages of the Bible can lie still in the quiet darkness with eyes closed while comforting words bring their ministry of peace to the tired body and spirit.

For many Psalm 23 will be a favorite choice. Others may prefer Psalms 8, 19, 24, 121. Other comforting passages for recall at this time are:

God is our refuge and strength, a very present help in trouble.
Therefore will not we fear, though the earth be removed, and though the mountains be carried into the midst of the sea;
Though the waters thereof roar and be troubled, though the mountains shake with the swelling thereof (Ps. 46:1–3).

O come, let us sing unto the Lord: let us make a joyful noise to the rock of our salvation. . . .
For the Lord is a great God, and a great King above all gods.
In his hand are the deep places of the earth: the strength of the hills is his also.
The sea is his, and he made it: and his hands formed the dry land.
O come, let us worship and bow down: let us kneel before the Lord our maker.
For he is our God; and we are the people of his pasture, and the sheep of his hand (Ps. 95:1, 3–7).

O Lord, thou hast searched me, and known me.
Thou knowest my downsitting and mine uprising, thou understandest my thoughts afar off.
Thou compassest my path and my lying down, and art acquainted with all my ways.
For there is not a word in my tongue, but, lo, O Lord, thou knowest it altogether.
Thou hast beset me behind and before, and laid thine hand upon me.
Such knowledge is too wonderful for me; it is high, I cannot attain unto it (Ps. 139:1–6).

18

The Home and the Church

One mark that distinguishes the Christian home from other homes in our modern American society is its relatedness to the redemptive fellowship of the Christian church. Let us hasten to avoid misunderstanding, however, by admitting that by no means are all church-related families also "redemptive fellowships." Obviously there are degrees, both quantitative and qualitative, of church-relatedness. Neither an individual nor a family can live a Christian life in isolation; the essence of Christianity is in human relationships.

The Loving Fellowship: "The Body of Christ"

Many attempts have been made to define the church of which each Christian family is a part and to describe its function, which the Christian family also shares. The genius of Paul caught its essence in a mere four words: "the body of Christ."

To be the body of Christ is a daring challenge. Even to think of this term applied to our individual lives is to be confronted with a sense of utter and complete failure. It seems like sacrilege. In his brief ministry Jesus set in motion forces that are changing the world. Even the most dedicated Christian, contrasting his life with that of Jesus, must shrink from the resulting revelation and must surely hear God's judgmental voice in his heart:

Look at the Man . . . and look at yourself!
Sons of the same Father, but who would dream it?
The firefly and the sun are no more unlike than you two.*

Each of us also needs the faith that can hear God's reassurance:

The firefly can't do anything about it. You can.
That's a part of the miracle of the soul . . .
    that the human creature can change, become
    different, grow out of the nature of the firefly,
    grow into the quality of the sun.
The worm and the moth, the cocoon and the butterfly,
    you—and what God wants you to be.*

"Ye are the body of Christ" (1 Cor. 12:27), wrote Paul. How
did he dare make this claim for the little group of first-century
Christians to whom he wrote? Were they perhaps very different
from us, much better people than we are? It seems unlikely. Paul
found many occasions to upbraid them. Listen to these verses from
an earlier chapter of the same letter.

Know ye not that the unrighteous shall not inherit the kingdom of
God? Be not deceived: neither fornicators, nor idolaters, nor adulterers,
nor effeminate, nor abusers of themselves with mankind,
    Nor thieves, nor covetous, nor drunkards, nor revilers, nor extor-
tioners, shall inherit the kingdom of God.
    And such were some of you: . . . (1 Cor. 6:9–11).

Quite ordinary people, apparently, even as were the twelve
disciples, and yet Paul dared to call them "the body of Christ."
Can there be some deeper meaning here not evident at first
glance? No one individual member of the fellowship would
dare apply to himself these words: "the body of Christ." Surely
the church is made up of its individual members and has no
separate existence apart from them, but is it perhaps true that
what would be sacrilege for any one of us alone may in some

strangely mysterious way be true of all of us together in the redemptive fellowship?

Each of us is capable at times of small bits of Christlike living. Each of us once in a while puts into practice the principles of living to which we give lip service. Each of us in rare moments lives by the law of love sufficiently to catch a glimpse of what true Christian living might be.

What if, in the marvelous economy of God, these rare bits of fumbling, "firefly" efforts can be gathered up and treasured and made to produce results far beyond our expectations or deserts? Once in a while we catch a glimpse of the mysterious way in which God magnifies the efforts of individuals.

Because some of us give a casual dollar to Church World Service, thousands of starving babies in distant lands are fed.

Because a few people become aware of lonely students from foreign lands living in their vicinity and make an effort to show friendliness, countless strong ties of friendship now reach across separating oceans into other lands.

Because a thirteen-year-old black American boy living in Italy reads about Albert Schweitzer and is moved with a great desire to help, a chain of events is started which results in a gift of medical supplies worth four hundred thousand dollars! [1]

Truly in these events we can see the body of Christ ministering to the needs of the world. They point up the importance of individual "firefly" ministries, the amazing way in which one person may be used of God to further his eternal purposes.

In a similar way the church itself has fulfilled its function as "the body of Christ" at work in the world. Fumblingly and imperfectly (like its individual members), it has struggled on, often guilty of denying the Christ it worships, frequently sinning against its own law of love, committing heinous crimes in the very name of religion, but somehow never completely losing its high vision of service. Repenting and receiving forgiveness, reforming only to sin again, it has somehow out of its travail brought forth new understandings, new visions, new dedication.

The church exists to be the body of Christ still carrying on his ministry in the world. The Christian family, as part of the church, shares in this responsibility.

Jesus' ministry consisted in totally giving himself to meet the needs of every person with whom he came in contact. Steadily, consistently, he gave himself, his strength, his courage, his faith, his love, to every last person, no matter how seemingly unimportant or unworthy. His giving of himself reached its climax in the death on the cross where he suffered the worst that evil could do in order to meet the needs of all mankind. He suffered to the end, still loving even those who killed him.

It is given to comparatively few of the faithful followers of Jesus through the ages to share his ministry of suffering and martyrdom. The lesser ministry of loving, self-forgetting service, of patient day-by-day doing of deeds of Christian love, has been carried on by uncounted thousands of "saints" in every generation.

The family in search of a winged faith, consistently trying to transform itself into a redemptive fellowship, will recognize itself as part of the greater fellowship, the Christian church, will participate in its corporate worship, and will share in its ministry to this fear-ridden, hate-filled world.

The "Church in Thy House"

In the exciting days when new little Christian churches were springing up along the routes of Paul's dangerous journeys, he wrote: "Paul . . . unto Philemon our dearly beloved, and fellowlabourer, . . . and to the church in thy house: Grace to you, and peace, from God our Father and the Lord Jesus Christ" (Philem. 1–3).

And again, in writing to the Corinthians: "Aquila and Priscilla salute you much in the Lord, with the church that is in their house" (1 Cor. 1:19). "The church in thy house," as it occurs in Paul's letters, refers of course to the little groups of Christians that met together in homes to worship and plan together and to share in the sacrament of the Lord's Supper long before there were any church buildings. William Barclay reminds us: "Nowhere in the New Testament does the word Church mean a building. . . . The Church is always a company of worshipping people who have given their hearts and pledged their lives to Jesus Christ.[2]

The church today is still people. The church is the church not just on Sunday morning when its members gather to worship. It is still the church on Monday and Tuesday and all through the week as its members carry on their daily lives in their homes and communities.

For us today, the phrase "the church in thy house" may come to have a more intimate meaning as we apply it to *our family. This* is "the church in thy house"! Grace to you and peace!

House Churches Today

One of the blessed ways in which the Holy Spirit is working in the church today is in the reestablishment and multiplication of "house churches" similar to those in the days of Paul. These are suddenly springing up in many scattered places, apparently as a part of the charismatic revival.

These house churches are not replacing the larger church fellowships but are proving a valuable adjunct to them. Frequently they take the form of a weekly prayer-and-praise meeting. In these small and intimate fellowships, many individual needs are revealed which are often lost in the regular church fellowships: needs for personal love and understanding, for further Bible study, for encouragement and growth in Christian insights, for resources to meet life in Christian ways.

The Christian home, extending its Christian ministry by opening its door to neighbors who are searching for the true "Rock" upon which to build their lives, will both be and receive a blessing.

Epilogue:

Waiting on the Lord

The ideal of a Christian family as a redemptive, Christ-centered fellowship can never be approached except by parents who have centered their living in dedication to Christ and have submitted themselves unreservedly to him and to his purpose for their lives. Here is one last encouraging word for parents seeking help for their daily walk. As you read and meditate upon it, may God open your hearts and minds that it may prove to you, as it has to me, a rich blessing!

They that wait on the Lord shall renew their strength; they shall mount up with wings as eagles; they shall run, and not be weary, they shall walk, and not faint (Isa. 40:31).

Yes, "they shall mount up with wings as eagles." You know what eagles' wings mean. The eagle is the king of birds, it soars the highest into the Heavens. . . .

You know how the eagles' wings are obtained. Only in one way—by the eagle birth. You are born of God. You *have* the eagles' wings. You may not have known it; you may not have used them; but God can and will teach you to use them.

You know how the eagles are taught the use of their wings. See yonder cliff rising a thousand feet out of the sea. See high up a ledge on the rock, where there is an eagles' nest with its treasure of two young eaglets. See the mother bird come and stir up her nest, and with her beak push the timid birds over the precipice. See how they flutter and fall and sink toward the depth. See now how she "fluttereth over her young, spreadeth abroad her wings, taketh them, beareth them on her wings" (Deut. 32:11), and so, as they ride upon her wings, brings them to a place of safety. And so she does once and again, each time casting them out over the precipice, and then again taking and carrying them. . . . The instinct of that eagle mother was God's gift, a single ray of that love in which the Almighty trains His people to mount as on eagles' wings.

He stirs up your nest. He disappoints your hopes. He brings down your confidence. He makes you fear and tremble as all your strength fails, and you feel utterly weary and helpless. And all the while He is spreading His strong wings for you to rest your weakness on, and offering His everlasting Creator-strength to work in you. And all He asks is that you should sink down in your weariness and *wait on Him;* and allow Him in His . . . strength to carry as you ride on the wings of His omnipotence.[1]

Notes

Chapter 1

1. From *The Christian Home in a Changing World* by Gene Getz, p. 40. Copyright 1972. Moody Press, Moody Bible Institute of Chicago. Used by permission.

2. Howard G. Hendricks, *Heaven Help the Home!* (Wheaton, Ill.: Victor Books, 1973), p. 63.

3. Slightly adapted from *The Book of Common Worship.* Copyright © 1946 by The Board of Christian Education of the Presbyterian Church in the United States of America. Used by permission.

Chapter 4

1. D. Elton Trueblood, *Alternative to Futility* (New York: Harper & Bros., 1948), p. 29.

Chapter 5

1. Margueritte Harmon Bro, *Every Day a Prayer* (Chicago: Willett, Clark, & Co., 1942), p. 94.

2. Samuel M. Shoemaker, *With the Holy Spirit and with Fire* (New York: Harper & Bros., 1960), p. 34.

Chapter 8

1. Larry Christenson, *The Christian Family* (Minneapolis, Minn.: Bethany Fellowship, 1970), p. 74.

Chapter 9

1. From *Your Child from Birth to Rebirth* by Anna B. Mow, pp. 111–112. Copyright © 1963 by Zondervan Publishing House, Grand Rapids, Michigan. Used by permission.

2. Ibid., pp. 107–8.

3. Hendricks, *Heaven Help the Home!,* pp. 70–72.

4. Ibid., pp. 76–77.

Chapter 10

1. From *Brethren, Hang Loose* by Robert Girard, pp. 206–7. Copyright © 1972 by The Zondervan Corporation, Grand Rapids, Michigan. Used by permission.

2. Part of the service of presentation of newborn babies used by the late Dr. George C. Vincent, for many years pastor of Union Congregational Church, Upper Montclair, New Jersey.

3. Mow, *Your Child,* p. 16.

Chapter 11
1. Copyright © 1970 by Dr. Thomas Gordon. From pp. 273–74 of *Parent Effectiveness Training: The Tested Way to Raise Responsible Children,* published by Peter H. Wyden, Inc. a division of David McKay Company, Inc. Reprinted by permission of the publisher.
2. Ibid., p. 274.
3. Ibid., pp. 191–93.

Chapter 12
1. Florence M. Taylor, *Their Rightful Heritage* (Boston: Pilgrim Press, 1942), pp. 13–14.
2. See Florence M. Taylor, *Hid in My Heart: The Word of God in Times of Need* (New York: Seabury Press, 1974).

Chapter 15
1. Harry Emerson Fosdick, *The Meaning of Service* (New York: Association Press, 1920), p. 162.
2. Bro, *Every Day a Prayer,* p. 152.

Chapter 16
1. From *Waiting on God,* by Andrew Murray, pp. 82–83. Copyright 1961. Moody Press, Moody Bible Institute of Chicago. Used by permission.
2. Ibid., pp. 83–86.
3. Georgia Harkness, *Prayer and the Common Life* (Nashville: Abingdon-Cokesbury Press, 1948), p. 13.

Chapter 17
1. From *From Everlasting to Everlasting: Promises and Prayers Selected from the Bible* by Florence M. Taylor, p. 112. Copyright © 1973. Used by permission of The Seabury Press.

Chapter 18
1. Morton Tuner, "To Dr. Schweitzer with Love," *Coronet,* April 1960.
2. William Barclay, *The Mind of St. Paul* (New York: Harper & Bros., 1958), pp. 237–38.

Epilogue
1. Murray, *Waiting on God,* pp. 105–8.

Suggested Reading

Brandt, Henry, and Landrum, Phil. *I Want to Enjoy My Children.* Grand Rapids, Mich.: Zondervan Publishing House, 1975.

Don't miss this one! Fascinating reading, and much deep wisdom and significant humor. Christian solutions for family crises.

Dreikurs, Rudolf, and Grey, Loren. *Logical Consequences:* New York: Meredith Press, 1968.

"The first step toward a new educational policy must be that one cannot hope for good results through punishment. It has to be replaced by the application of logical or natural consequences where the child is impressed with the needs of reality and not with the power of the adult" (p. 42).

Getz, Gene. *The Christian Home in a Changing World.* Chicago: Moody Press, 1972.

"There is only one perspective that will enable men and women to find answers to the perplexing problems facing them in their married and family life. It is the biblical perspective. Apart from God's love and principles as revealed in Scripture, there is no safe way to determine ultimate and enduring answers" (p. 9).

Girard, Robert C. *Brethren, Hang Loose.* Grand Rapids, Mich.: Zondervan Publishing House, 1972.

See quotations on page 82.

Gordon, Thomas. *Parent Effectiveness Training: The Tested Way to Raise Responsible Children.* New York: Peter H. Wyden, Inc., 1970.

This book is highly recommended; it is sound psychologically and full of rich examples of both futile and effective ways of handling parent-child relationships. The Christian parent will find here an illuminating source of deeper understanding of his children and of himself but will recognize that the book makes no pretense of presenting these insights in a specifically Christian context. Much of its approach is based upon religious values—respect for the child's personality, acceptance of the child as he is, and so on. Christian parents, however, will recognize the necessity of enriching the family life with genuine experiences of worship and study of God's Word, *in order to achieve* the desirable parent-child relationships described. See quotations on pages 90–92.

Hendricks, Howard G. *Heaven Help the Home!* Wheaton, Ill.: Victor Books, 1973.

An excellent and readable book on "the art and joy of successful family living." Bears the interesting dedication: "To Barb, Bob, Bev, and Bill—the four arrows God placed in my quiver, uncommonly gifted as my personal instructors in parenthood. See quotations on pages 25, 75.

Mow, Anna B. *Your Child From Birth To Rebirth.* Grand Rapids, Mich.: Zondervan Publishing House, 1963.

See quotations on pages 74, 84–85.

Murray, Andrew. *How to Raise Your Children for Christ.* Minneapolis, Minn.: Bethany Fellowship, 1975.

"To all parents who truly long to have their homes truly consecrated by God's presence and service, God's Word has a message of comfort and strength. It is this: God is willing to be the God of their home, and with His divine power will do more than they can ask and think. If they will but open their hearts in faith to rest in the promise and power of god. . . ." (Preface).

Narramore, Bruce. *Help I'm a Parent: A Guide to Child Rearing.* Grand Rapids, Mich.: Zondervan Publishing House, 1972.

"The Bible gives a great foundation for the parent-child relation. It also serves as a corrective force to balance the whims of current psychological theory. By combining the practical insights of modern psychology with the lasting truths of the Bible, we have a solid and balanced approach to the problems of the modern parent" (p. 7).

————. *An Ounce of Prevention: A Parent's Guide to Moral and Spiritual Growth of Children.* Grand Rapids, Mich.: Zondervan Publishing House, 1973.

"When we're going on a journey, we get a map. We have a goal in mind, and we make periodic checks on our progress. Likewise, Christian training is a journey. We pass through various stages, and need directions at various times. To be sure we arrive at our chosen destination we need to map out goals in family living. Then we must make periodic checks to be sure we're making needed progress" (p. 37).